THE 25 RUPEES I DIDN'T GET MADE ME WHAT I AM

BOUNCING FORWARD BY TRANSFORMING POSSIBILITIES INTO SUCCESS

JOEL D'SOUZA

Made with ♥ on the Notion Press Platform
www.notionpress.com

This book is dedicated to all those who have experienced hurt, rejections, but dared to hope, took risks, conquered fear and dared to live.

You are the proof that light will always prevail.

Contents

Foreword

Enter the world of Joel D'Souza - my Friend, Technocrat, Entrepreneur, Business Trainer and now an Author - where each page of his book unveils a journey of resilience, revelation, and remarkable transformation. Through candid storytelling, Joel bares his soul, sharing the highs and lows of his path from adversity to entrepreneurial success.

In these pages, Joel invites you to witness the evolution of his mindset - a shift that propelled him from setbacks to fulfillment. His story is a testament to the power of perspective, illustrating how embracing challenges can lead to profound personal growth and achievement.

More than just a memoir, Joel's narrative is a beacon of inspiration, emphasizing the value of giving back, authenticity, and impacting lives. From his humble beginnings as a door-to-door salesman to his role as a revered entrepreneur and a business trainer, Joel's journey is a testament to the transformative potential within us all. As you delve into Joel's unique writing style, you will discover the timeless principles that guided him through adversity and toward purpose. Each turn of the page offers not only insight but also the promise of newfound joy and fulfillment.

With heartfelt wishes for Joel's continued success, may his story ignite a flame of aspiration within each one of you. Embrace his words with an open heart and mind, for within them lies the power to catalyze positive change and unlock the full potential of your own journey.

Maxson Lewis

Founder & CEO, Magenta Mobility

CHAPTER ONE

THE MIND CODING

Have you ever come across people who are unhappy, frustrated, confused, with no clarity or focus in life, stuck with a 9 to 5 job or a stagnant business which they don't like?

Such people are easy to find, isn't it? Most of them have loans piled up on them and their lives revolve around the EMIs (Equated Monthly Installments). Their frustration and confused state destroys their personal lives, family lives and relationships. Rather than living their lives, they *spend* their lives in these problematic whirlpools which they themselves have created.

Ask yourself honestly - Are you one of them? Is any of your family members one of them? Then you or they are one of those whose minds have been coded from infancy for creating problems and then running aimlessly to solve them.

Remember, you cannot solve a problem with the same mindset that you have created it. You need to change your game to get to the next level to understand the problem and solve it.

Life is all about how we respond to situations that comes across. Our responses to it will define the outcomes. So it's plain to see that our happiness depends upon ourselves and no one else. Schooling, job, business, relationships, parenting etc. are all by-products of life. These by-products are created the way we do it. What we actually want out of it may differ from the way we do it. The doing process depends upon how our brains have been coded through our formative years. Mind is coded and is set when something is done repeatedly, for a long period of time, without CONSCIOUSLY changing WHAT and HOW it is done. That's how MINDSET is formed!

As early as I can remember, my childhood was fairly decent. My father Daniel was working for a reputed MNC as a Service Technician for switchgears and circuit breakers. He had a typical 8 to 5 job and also used to travel often across the country as a part of his job.

My father and my mother Leena came from 2 different small villages near Brahmavar, a small town near Mangalore in Karnataka, India. After my father completed his 10th grade, he moved to Mumbai (then Bombay) and joined the company where his elder brother was working. For a paradigm shift of village life to city life, a lot of adjustments had to be made. All these adjustments were made in the way his mind was coded in the typical village setup, education and strict parenting. He got married to a girl from another village near Mangalore, a simple woman whose mind again was coded in the typical village setup, education and strict parenting. Both had tough times in their childhood. Working in the fields, walking about 5 kilometers one way barefoot to school, one meal a day was just a few of them. After 3 years of their marriage, I was the firstborn, my siblings being a brother Allen and a sister

Benita.

While my father was most of the times away travelling at work on company tours or with responsibilities in our religion of Jehovah's Witnesses handling our local congregation, it was our mother who did most of the parenting to us.

My father never attempted changing his job since it gave him all the comfort and time for his other activities. He eventually retired from the same company after working for 43 years.

My mother taught us the values of fearing God, doing things honestly and all the other things which are part of regular parenting. Since my father was very strict, my mother, I and my siblings were extremely scared of him. Most of the times, his fear kept us from doing what we wanted to do. Sometimes that fear proved to be helpful and sometimes the other way around. We were not allowed in any school extra-curricular activities, be it the annual day program, sports or school picnic. Our association with friends was very limited inculcating the fear in us that all these things will result in bad for us. It was in such situations I grew up, and my mind was coded for fear. Fear was the basis of my life. Whatever I would do or not, was because of the fear in me and the way my mind was coded. I was an average student sometimes failing in a few subjects in school, resulting in very heavy discipline and beatings from my father. So the lines of fear were very clearly drawn in my life. As the eldest son, a lot was expected from me.

Even at school, the focus was only on marks and not creativity. We were being coded to become machines working for others. Strict teachers and their needless discipline at times made it all the more difficult for me.

I was doing nothing by my own interest or creativity since it was all curbed and dead inside me. Everything that I did was only out of fear! My parents or teachers did not do anything different. This is what parenting and schooling was all about those days and even now.

Why am I talking so much on mind coding?

Because if there's anything called magic, it's in there, in YOUR MIND!

Although all are born equal - with empty pages, to be filled as life goes through, your dreams and the ability to sustain your dreams and lives are different. *Whatever you believe, you will achieve.* So if you are coded negatively and with fear, it lets you believe that you are a loser. But if you believe that you will be successful or otherwise, then you will be.

Your mind has two components – the conscious and the subconscious. The conscious mind is responsible for everything you see, hear or experience at any given moment. But it plays a very small role in realizing your dreams. It is your subconscious mind that has the ability to work out wonders. But your subconscious mind needs to be trained to work out wonders. You need to feed your subconscious mind through your conscious mind. What you put in, is what you get. With great skills of your mind, your great mind puts your great abilities to use.

The way you feel within is what your life outside will be. It's all in the mind!

You got to take 100% personal responsibility of your life. You cannot change the weather, the seasons, circumstances, or the wind, but you can change *yourself*.

It is time to stop looking for outside yourself for the answers to why you haven't created the life and results you want, for it is you who creates the quality of the life you lead and the results you produce. You have to give up all your excuses. 99% of all failures come from people who have a habit of making excuses. Learn to get in touch with the silence within yourself and know that everything in life has a purpose.

Decide your major definite purpose in life and then organize all your activities around it.

Believe that it's possible. You can be anything you want to be, if only you believe with sufficient conviction and *act* in accordance with your faith, for whatever your mind can conceive and believe, your mind can achieve. Believe in yourself and go for it.

You have to give up "I can't." These words are the most powerful force of negation in the human psyche. Don't waste your life believing you can't. What others think of you is none of your business.

Self-belief is more powerful and more important than any other form of external validation or approval by other people.

Your life is too short to dwell on what you failed to achieve or to do that will not lead to success.

Sooner or later, those who win are those who think they can.

Your conditioned mind creates mental barriers around you.
You become enslaved to such invisible barriers and live in self denial of such slavery.
Beware with what you condition your mind with and with whom you surround yourself with.

– Joel D'Souza

CHAPTER TWO

REJECTION - WHAT'S THAT?

As I grew up, my first big achievement in my life was to learn cycling when I was 9 years. It was the 1st defining moment of my life. Renting out bicycles hourly and taking it for long rides was like kicking my spirit alive. The relative freedom I experienced was priceless! Though I was restricted by my parents from riding the bicycle outside our apartment lane, the fact that they could not supervise me there, gave me my chance to taste my own interest. During vacations, it became a routine to rent out bicycles which though in bad shape gave me immense joy riding them.

Simultaneously, I started pestering my father, through my mother of course, to buy me a bicycle. My parents always used to tell me how dangerous it is for small children to ride bicycles as accidents keep happening. They tried to put fear in me. Though out of love for me, their intentions were right but unknowingly they were curbing my growth. Also considering our financial situation, it was difficult for my father to buy one as it was a huge cost for him then. Eventually after 4 years of convincing him, my father bought me Hero Ranger Senior bicycle for the princely amount of Rs. 1,010 then. That was the happiest day of my life till then. My excitement and happiness knew no bounds and all the discipline and beatings I got from my dad were forgiven then! Buying a bicycle for me though came with a rider – no riding it outside our apartment lane! Again fear! Again limitations! Again curbing of my instincts!

Nevertheless, the relative freedom I got after getting my bicycle made me explore more without of course letting my parents come to know about it. I started riding it across the town and also to other towns nearby. I used to love those rides, the best part of my life so far!

After vacations when school started in the rainy season, the lanes near our apartment used to get flooded. Riding my bicycle in those flooded roads was even more fun. It was like living my dream. Eventually riding on flooded roads took a toll on my bicycle. It became hard & rough to ride, and that is the time I learnt, it needs to be serviced. I went to a bicycle repair shop across my school and came to know the service cost was 25 rupees! I came home and asked my mother 25 rupees which she was unable to give. The following month she saved from the groceries money that my father used to give her and she gave that 25 rupees. I immediately went to the bicycle repair shop and told them to service my bicycle. The elderly gentleman there told me that 25 rupees is just the service labor cost. He went on to tell that during service all the ball bearings need to be changed, grease and oil is required for which another 25 rupees would be charged. I was in a fix now! My beloved bicycle was not running well, it needed service! I asked my mother for another 25 rupees, and she rejected! Though she really wanted to give the 25 rupees, I understood that it was simply beyond her monthly budget. I was heart-broken and tearfully accepted her reality but not the rejection. I did not give up. I eventually got what I wanted.

What helped me get over this rejection?

I rejected REJECTION. To get over rejection, you have to realize that rejection is really a myth. It doesn't really exist. It is simply an idea that you hold in your head. Think about it. If you ask a girl to have dinner with you and she says no, you didn't have anyone to eat dinner with before you asked her, and you don't have anyone to eat dinner with after you asked her. Did the situation change? No, it stayed the same.

When you encounter rejection you should keep going back stronger, not weaker, because you have not allowed rejection to beat you down. It will only keep strengthening your resolve. To be successful there is no other way. It takes courage to know who you are and what you stand for. It takes courage to act from the core of your own being -- your core essence. Learning how to deal effectively with rejection strengthens your sense of self and builds your resilience when confronting life's challenges.

Get used to the fact that there is going to be a lot of rejection along the way in life.

The secret to success is to not give up. When someone says no, you just say, *"Ok, Next!"* Keep on asking. Find out options; think your next possible moves. If one person tells you no, ask someone else, try something else. Don't get demotivated or get stuck in your fear or resentment. Just move on - to the next person or the next thing or the next option.

You reach a higher dimension when you reject rejection, ignore small talks, ignore the noise around you and focus only on your goals. The freedom you experience in this dimension will propel you towards your goals.

– Joel D'Souza

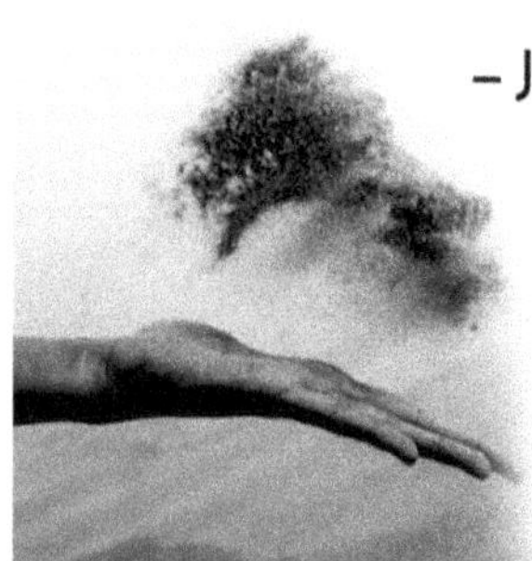

CHAPTER THREE

DON'T JUST BE A POSITIVE THINKER, BE A POSSIBILITY THINKER

Possibility is what you don't know, the unknown, what is beyond your current thoughts, words and actions. So if you believe something is impossible, don't hesitate, just do it. Over a period of time, this possibility thinking in any situation will become coded in your mind.

So what is it that differentiates Possibility Thinkers from Positive Thinkers? The only difference is that Possibility Thinkers operate from the thoughts of no constraints – constraints of anything, be it time, money, resources etc. do not exist for them and they find alternate ways of doing things, irrespective of any kind of limitations.

Because they know that only thinking positive is not enough, they just go ahead and do it, digging inside their deepest capabilities. As an established fact, the true character and caliber of a person emerges only when he or she is pushed beyond their limits of comfort zones and their true worth is tested. Successful people are created out of ordinary people.

Possibility Thinkers have no connection with age, health and wealth of an individual. It is a game of the mind, for the mind, in the mind, it's their vision, a permanent phenomenon which only ends with life.

Ask yourself –

If I think that there is something that is impossible to do in my life today, and yet it could be done, would it fundamentally change my life?

If I think that there is something that is impossible to do in my business today, and yet it could be done, would it fundamentally change my business?

Since my father was a service technician of switchgears and circuit breakers, he had a whole lot of tools at home. These tools used to fascinate me. So after 2 days of drooling over not getting the additional 25 rupees – I moved beyond positive thinking to a possibility thinker. I decided to use the tools that I had at home and service my bicycle myself. Next day after school I went to the bicycle repair shop and saw in detail how a bicycle is serviced. I spent about 3 hours watching what kinds of tools are used, where the grease and oil is applied, which place and which size ball bearings are fixed etc. I went home, checked the tools I had at home and figured out I had all those that are required. Next day I went back to the bicycle repair shop and purchased the grease, oil and 2 different sizes of ball bearings with the original 25 rupees which my mother had given me.

Following Sunday, I carried my bicycle up to my home, took it to the balcony, flipped it upside down and started something *that would lay a foundation for my life ahead.*

With great difficulty and with hurting myself I opened up the wheels, handle, axle, brakes, pedals etc. using spanners, screw drivers and other tools. Systematically fixed the ball bearings with the grease and oil after cleaning the area, I lubricated all the joints, chain, sprocket etc. and fixed the parts back. When I first tried the bicycle post my operation on it, I realized the rear wheel was jammed. It wasn't moving. I was too tired to try doing anything again that day. Next day I went to bicycle repair shop and I told the old man there about my predicament. That old man was happy to see my efforts and told me that I have over torqued the rear axle, loosen it a bit and it will be fine. I came home and did exactly what the old man said, took the bicycle on the road and whoa - the bicycle was all smooth and fast. I washed it with soap water to get rid of all the grease and oil marks and the bicycle was as new as it was when it was brought home the first day. This was the 2nd defining moment of my life. So effectively, ***the additional 25 rupees that I didn't get from my mother then made me what I am today.*** How and what, we will know as we move ahead.

Do you see the Possibility Thinker here?

Possibility thinkers are great risk takers.
For them nothing is impossible.
– Joel D'Souza
JD Talks

CHAPTER FOUR

FEEL THE FEAR AND DO IT ANYWAY

When I started it, I never ever thought that I would complete it successfully. But I didn't give in to the fear of assuming I would fail. Since I had never done it before, it was too difficult for me as a 13 year old to use tools for the first time and do something that I had no evidence of success. But I completed it successfully. I rejected rejection and fear, and thought about the possible option. I just went ahead and did it.

As you move ahead on your journey to achieve what you want, you are going to face fears and you have to confront those fears. Fear is natural. Whenever you start anything new, it starts with fear - be it business or relationship or anything else. Successful people, on the other hand feel the fear as the rest of us, but they don't let it keep them from doing anything they want to do or have to do. They understand that fear is something to be acknowledged, experienced, and taken along for the ride.

You have to be willing to feel the fear.

Some people will do anything to avoid the uncomfortable feeling of fear. If you are one of those people, you run an even bigger risk of never getting what you want in life.

Psychologists say that F E A R means False Evidences Appearing Real.

To help you better understand how you actually bring unfounded fear into your life; make a list of the things you are afraid to do. This is not a list of things you are afraid of, such as being afraid of spiders, but things you are afraid to do, such as being afraid to pick up a spider. For example, I am afraid to -

- To drive
- Ask the girl/boy you love out for a date
- Leave my kids with a baby sitter
- Leave this job that I hate

Now go back and restate each fear using the following format –

I want to ______________________ and I scare myself by imagining ____________________.

The key words are *I scare myself by imagining.* All fear is self-created by imagining some negative outcome of the future. Using some of the same fear listed above, the new format would look like this –

1. I want to drive, and I scare myself by imagining the traffic and heavy vehicles than can come around me.
2. I want to ask my love out for a date, and I scare myself by imagining that he/she would say no and I would feel embarrassed.

3. I want to leave my baby with a baby sitter, and I scare myself by imagining that something terrible would happen to him/her.
4. I want to leave this job that I hate to pursue my dream, and I scare myself by imagining I would go bankrupt and lose my house.

Do you realize that it's you that is creating the fear?

Remember there is no failure, only feedback.

So do not fear feedback that helps to better you.

A small child learning to walk often falls, not once, but many times. As a learning process, it's inevitable. Have you ever heard a child that has learnt to walk without falling? Yet when a person tries to do something and fails, we label him or her a failure. This is wrong. The person is not a failure. It's only his or her actions that have failed.

The truth is that for every win which you see there are hundreds or thousands of failed attempts that you don't see.

It takes courage to look at your failed attempts, acknowledge them, count them, learn from them but not allow them to overwhelm you. The key to success lies in how you emotionally respond to the result of your decisions and actions. If they don't produce the desired result, it should energize you to try again, this time with more experience.

When you experience failure, do not apply that label to yourself. When you fail, do not take it to heart, take it as a feedback for your decisions and actions, analyze it and figure out why your decisions and actions did not produce the desired results. Once you have realized where you went wrong, your realization is your feedback.

HOW TO MAKE YOUR FEARS VANISH? One way to actually make your fear vanish is to ask yourself what you are imagining that you are so scared of, and then replace that visualization with its positive opposite visualization.

Replace the physical sensations that fear brings. Focus on the physical sensations you are currently feeling – sensations you are probably just identifying as fear and then focus on those feelings you would like to be experiencing instead – courage, self-confidence, calm, joy.

Fix these two different impressions firmly in your visualizations and then slowly go back and forth between the two, spending about 15 seconds in each one. After a minute or two, the fear will vanish and you will find yourself in a neutral, centered and a calm place.

I learnt and mastered the skill of bicycle repairs and then every six months I used to open up my bicycle and completely overhaul it myself. It made me proud of myself that I didn't need anyone's help to do it. My curiosity and thirst for learning and fascination with tools made me learn the basics of plumbing, carpentry and electrical work. The fear of an electric shock or anything that could go wrong didn't stop me. From the age of 14 onwards, I was doing all maintenance activities for my home and that of my neighbors which included, changing taps, changing switches, repairing damaged furniture. I even repaired a special ice making refrigerator which was one of its kind in my neighboring apartment for which I earned a sum of Rs. 51! ***All this because of the 25 rupees I didn't get!***

I learnt riding 2 wheelers and driving 4 wheelers by myself and by the age of 14, I was comfortable riding my neighbors' scooter and my grandfather's Ambassador Car. I developed a passion for cars and started picking automobile magazines to feed my passion and keeping myself abreast of all new cars and its features. ***Sometime during this period, I dreamt of having my own car workshop.*** The idea then was very vague but I knew I had to do it. I started day dreaming about it, the visualization of a car workshop was taking shape in my mind.

Remember when you won in the face of fear. If you can remember that experience or the first time you rode a two wheeler or drove a car, you have got the model for everything that happens in life. New experiences will always feel a little scary. They are supposed to. That's the way it works. But every time you face a fear and do it anyway, you build up that much more confidence in your abilities.

Anthony Robbins says "If you can't, you must, and if you must, you can".

It is those very things that we are most afraid to do that provide the greatest freedom and growth for us. Master the skills you need to learn, move through your fears, and then take on bigger challenges.

Don't let the fear of failing stop you.

Fear of 'what people will say'
Fear of 'consequences of your right actions'
Fear of 'losing your assumed great name with fake people'
Fear of 'losing a position of authority or opportunity'
Fear of 'risks'
Fear of 'the unseen future'

Fear - man's greatest enemy,
befriended by majority!

– Joel D'Souza

JD Talks

CHAPTER FIVE

FEEL THE PAIN, TAKE ACTION

BE WILLING TO PAY THE PRICE

Pain is only momentary, temporary, but the benefits last forever. It's not the will to win that matters – everyone has that. It's the will to *prepare* to win that matters. You need to put in the time and efforts. Part of paying the price is the willingness to do whatever it takes to get the job done. It comes from a declaration that you are going to get it done no matter what it takes, no matter how long it takes, no matter what comes up. It's a done deal. You are responsible for the results you intend. No excuses – just a world class performance or an outstanding result that can be counted on.

Talent is cheaper than table salt. What separates the talented individual from the successful one is a lot of hard work and determination. Creating momentum is an important part of the success process. In fact, successful people know that if you are willing to pay the price in the beginning you can reap the benefits for the rest of your life. Indian Cricketer Vinod Kambli was equally talented as his team mate Master blaster Sachin Tendulkar. They both played together for their school and even for India. Sachin's immense success was because of his dedication, hard work, focus and the countless hours he spent on preparing for games. Vinod Kambli just faded in oblivion as little bit of early success went to his mind, he lost his focus and faltered.

TAKE ACTION

Things may come to those who wait, but only the things left by those who hustle.

Your thoughts, your knowledge or your beliefs, in the end are of no value. You get value with what you do with it! The world doesn't pay you for what you know; it pays you for what you do.

The only thing that separates winners from losers more than anything else is - winners take action.

They simply get up and do what has to be done. Once they have developed a plan, they start. They get into motion. Even if they don't start perfectly, they learn from their mistakes, make the necessary corrections, and keep taking action, all the time building momentum, until they finally produce the result they set out to produce or something even better than they conceived of when they started. Nothing happens until you take action.

So quit waiting! It's time to quit waiting for perfection, inspiration, permission, reassurance, someone to change, the right person to come along, the kids to grow, the new government to take over, an absence of risk, someone to discover you, a clear set of instructions, more self-confidence, the pain to go away.

Get on with it already. Satisfaction comes from enough action. Fail forward - no man has ever become great or good except through many and great mistakes.

I found college life too boring, I hardly attended college. Books and classroom learning never excited me. So I simultaneously found my first job while in college. It was purely on commission basis and there was no salary. My job was to sell microwave proof plastic containers. My sales depot was far off and I had to pick up stuff from there and go to premium areas of the city to sell it. The rude behavior of many in those areas didn't dampen my spirit. One of the days, I was in an area very close to my relatives' house. So I went to meet them. When they saw me with this big bag and the containers in it, they just laughed at me. It was a ridicule which I could not take and I walked off from there.

For 2 months I worked extremely hard and I tried my best to sell the containers, but I couldn't! I hardly sold 4-5 pieces in 2 months after which I had to quit! My mother gave me money every day to cover my travel and food expenses. She thought I wasted that money, but I knew I was learning something priceless in the University of Life! With all this, I never gave up buying those automobile magazines and feed my passion.

Then while in college I pursued a Diploma in Computer Engineering. The thought of assembling computers, opening it up excited me since I could get to work with tools. I finished the 1 year diploma with a reputed institute and after 12th grade, started working as a Trainee Customer Support Executive with a company in Mumbai. Simultaneously I enrolled in Mumbai University Distant Education program to complete my further studies. My first salary was here was 800 rupees and my travel allowance 300 rupees. For 6 months, I worked hard and the foundation for my career was laid here. 300 rupees allowance used to finish in the first 10 days of the month. I used to walk across the streets of Mumbai and its suburbs with a heavy bag full of tools and the support kit. After 6 months I landed with a same kind of new job but with a salary of 3,000 rupees and 800 rupees as travel allowance. I wasn't too concerned about my low salary, but I was getting to know people with different backgrounds, see new places, experience the grind that life takes you through in this city, travelling in the crowded trains and buses made my life more interesting. I used to reach home very late in the nights after attending customer calls. Once my father did not take me home as I reached home somewhere around 1 a.m. I literally slept on our apartment stairs. My father being in an 8 to 5 job all his life never understood my job profile. He was like the frog in the well who thought all jobs were just like his, in a closed world. Such incidents only helped me with my determination to make it count. During these years, I was least bothered about my university studies but was getting my PhD from the University of Life. I don't even know whether I cleared S.Y. B.Com exams since I never went to university to collect my results.

By the age of 20, I was a university drop out with 2 years of experience in computer hardware, working in a computer manufacturing company travelling across the city and suburbs attending customer calls, reaching home late in the night with the fear of my father's anger. During this time, I quit my job and started my first business with 2 of my friends of assembling computers and selling and taking up maintenance contracts. My friends who were computer hardware engineers didn't leave their jobs since they were afraid of the business not working well and losing their jobs. I was the driving force behind the business. I got orders for new computers and maintenance contracts. Unfortunately, I had to close down the business with no support from my friends as they were not ready to quit their jobs. So my first business was a total failure, but gave me a feedback - what works, what doesn't. What I went through all this was the awkward phase of my life. I failed forward. Even in such situations, my passion and curiosity for automobiles was very much alive and I kept feeding it through whatever resources possible.

Going through the awkward stage

Remember when you first learned to ride a bicycle, drive a car, or to play a sport? You understood in advance that you were going to be very awkward at first. You assumed that awkward was just part of what was required to learn that new skill that you wanted.

But to gain a new skill or get better at anything you want to do, you have to be willing to keep on going in the face of looking foolish and feeling stupid for a time.

SUCCESS IS 10% INSPIRATION AND 90% PERSPIRATION

Planning has its place, but it must be kept in perspective. Some people spend their whole lives waiting for the perfect time to do something. There's rarely a perfect time to do anything. What is important is to just get started. Get into the game. Get on the playing field. Once you do you will start to get feedback that will help you make the corrections you need to make to be successful. Once you are in action, you will start learning at a much more rapid rate.

Many people fail to take action because they are afraid to fail. Successful people on the other hand, realize that failure is an important part of the learning process. They know that failure is just a way we learn by trial and error. Not only do we need to stop being so afraid of failure but we also need to be willing to fail – even eager to fail. Fail forward. Simply get started, make mistakes, listen to the feedback, correct, and keep moving forward toward the goal. Every experience will yield up more useful information that you can apply the next time. You can never learn less, you can only learn more.

Do not look for endorsements from others – People who are successful are loners in their journey. They are self-contained, self-sufficient, independent individuals who are confident of their actions and works with their solitary thought process, independent of support, backing or approval of the world in what they feel is right. Not seeking endorsement is not an act of arrogance, but successful people know that their ideas will be shot down by the world and they will be asked to toe the line with the philosophies that the world believes in.

After closing down my first business, I was quite disappointed. But my mistake was to look for outside validation for myself and my ideas. I was looking to seek endorsement from my friends to keep my business running. By the time I realized it, it was too late. But I kept my learning from it and moved on.

Thanks to the push my aunty Julie gave to my uncle Boniface, my mother's elder brother, he arranged for a visa to the UAE. I went to Dubai looking for a job. I got a decent job in the 5th month of my stay there. The company was a startup catering to the Retail IT industry. I joined there as a customer support executive. Life took a back seat and what started was a dignified slavery in the UAE. All my aspirations, dreams shattered when I realized that the company was not doing well and we had problems getting our salaries. Changing job was not an option there since I was bound by a 3 year contract and so I call it dignified slavery. Life went on with all the struggles. Fortunately I was staying with my other uncle named Denis and his wife named Gloria and I didn't have many expenses. Boniface uncle, Denis uncle and Gloria aunty looked after me as their own son. I got my driving license in Dubai at the first test which is very rare even now. I got married at the age of 25 in India to a girl named Lydia whom I dated for 7 years. My wedding to her was my 3rd defining moment in my life. Lydia joined me in Dubai and we moved to a separate rented apartment.

The month Lydia joined me in Dubai, I did not get my salary. We didn't have money even to eat food during that month. Whatever little savings were there after spending a fortune for our wedding in Mumbai, was spent in renting the house in Dubai and putting basic things into it. We survived eating bread and butter since that was the only thing we could eat on credit which the local small grocery store gave us. It was an extremely difficult period for me that questioned my self-worth and my abilities. But with the help of some friends and my uncle and aunt, we survived that phase. My wife landed up with a good job and I changed my job after finishing my contract. Life went on. We both were working, money was coming, we bought a 2 BHK flat in a prominent place in Pune in India with the help of a bank loan, and weekends were spent with friends and some relatives. Since I satiated my thirst for driving premium and exotic cars in Dubai, somehow the vicious circle of life took me away from my passion of automobiles.

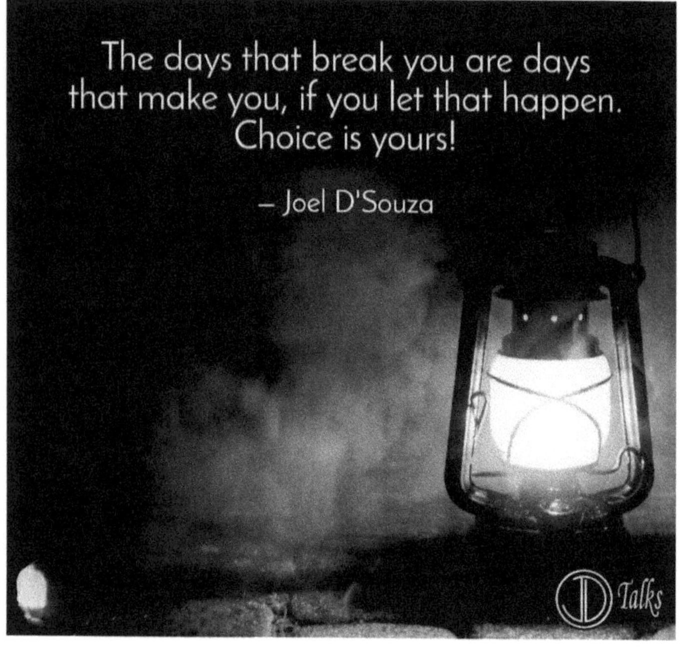
The days that break you are days
that make you, if you let that happen.
Choice is yours!
– Joel D'Souza
JD Talks

CHAPTER SIX

GET OUT OF YOUR COMFORT ZONE

Life for me from outside looked sorted & great! We had good jobs. We could afford renting a good house. We had a good car. We had great friends. I was in my comfort zone now whereas the reality was that I had got entangled in the whirlpool of life trying to make my future secure living through my insecurities!

Life actually begins at the end of your comfort zone.

The life of a content person is solidly comfortable. And comfort kills growth. Discontinuity is necessary. When we want to do something new we usually pick the safe choice.

Most people drive through life with their psychological emergency brake on. They hold on to negative images about themselves or suffer the effects of powerful experiences they haven't yet released. They stay in a comfort zone entirely of their own making. They maintain inaccurate beliefs about reality or harbor guilt and self-doubt. And when they try to achieve their goals, these negative images and preprogrammed comfort zones always cancel out their good intentions – no matter how hard they try.

Successful people, on the other hand, have discovered that instead of using increased willpower as the engine to power their success, it's simply easier to release the brakes by letting go of and replacing their limiting beliefs and changing their self-images. Perhaps you have even been trained to limit yourself.

Perhaps this also describes you - still trapped in a comfort zone by something as puny and weak as the small rope and stake that controls the elephant, except your rope is made up of the limiting beliefs and images that you received and took on when you were young. If this describes you, the good news is that you can change your comfort zone. How? There are three different ways:

- You can use affirmations and positive self-talk to affirm already having what you want, doing what you want and being the way you want.
- You can create powerful and compelling new internal images of having, doing, and being what you want.
- You can simply change your behavior.

As long as you keep complaining about your present circumstances, your mind will focus on it. By continually talking about, thinking about, and writing about the ways things are, you are continually reinforcing those very same neural pathways in your brain that got you to where you are today. And you are continually sending out the same vibrations that will keep attracting the same people and circumstances that you have already created.

The significant problems we face cannot be solved by the same level of thinking that created them.
– Albert Einstein

Every time you are making a choice, one choice is the safe/comfortable choice, and one choice is the risky/ uncomfortable choice. The risky/uncomfortable choice is the one that will teach you the most and make you grow the most, so that's the one you should choose. Remember that tomorrow is a new day. It helps to remember that what doesn't kill you generally really does make you stronger — you will survive, you will heal, you will learn something, you will have a better chance of emerging unscathed next time.

So change before you have to. Any change brings with it a lot of fear, insecurities, difficulties, pain, sacrifice and risk.

When you are at the crest of seemed success and decide to change, you don't feel the difficulty or the pain because the change that you are initiating is largely self-driven and self- initiated. It is not driven by the external things. It is not forced upon you. If a change is forced half your energy and passion is lost in resisting the change, saying no to that new idea and you will never experience its true potential as you won't allow the power of the idea to sink in. you will fail to take advantage of the opportunity. Therefore change before you have to.

As our seemingly good life was going on in routine, I came to know that my wife was expecting our first child. Suddenly, we had to make a decision.

Much to my wife's resistance, I decided to change tracks and get out of my comfort zone. Despite the home loan EMI hovering over my head, I decided to move back to India and start working there and raise our kid in India. So I made her quit her job, cancelled her visa and we came back to India. I didn't quit my job as I thought I will work for another year in the UAE, save some money and then move back. But life had other plans. When I came to Mumbai on a short vacation, I saw an advertisement of a vacant job profile in Pune, a city about 180 kilometers away from Mumbai, which matched my skills and experience. I immediately applied for it and was called by the CEO, Susil Dungarwal, for an interview. Susil Dungarwal is one of the well-known faces of the Indian retail industry.

I cleared all the rounds of the interview and returned back to the UAE waiting for the offer letter. In a few days I got the offer letter and the remuneration figures were there for my satisfaction. I accepted the offer and within a month I was happy to be back to India. Since we had bought a 2 BHK apartment in Pune, we decided to settle down in Pune. My son Leander was born in the second month of my new job in Pune. This was my life's 4th defining moment. We were happy to be back to India in our own house and with a good job. The subsequent 8 years that I spent in my Pune was a period of 2 extremes. Some great things happened in my life and some worst too. We will consider these in the following pages.

Once we moved to Pune, I purchased a used car and the desire to play with it technically with all the knowledge I had gathered tempted me a lot.

A year after my job in Pune, I got promoted 3 levels at one go, thanks to my boss Tushar Mehta (who had replaced Susil Dungarwal as the CEO) who also became my close friend and my mentor. I qualified for a company car which made me happy because now I could experiment with my own car. Subsequently I did a lot of technical adjustments in the car, and it was like a rocket on the road. Even though in the UAE, I lost track of my passion, I resurrected it as soon as I got back to India. I fueled my passion for cars now with working on my own car and being successful with what I intended to do.

FUEL YOUR SUCCESS WITH PASSION AND ENTHUSIASM

Enthusiasm is one of the most powerful engines of success. Be active, be energetic, be enthusiastic and faithful, and you will accomplish your object. Nothing great was ever achieved without enthusiasm.

BE FILLED WITH PASSION

No doubt you know or have met people who are passionate about life and enthusiastic about their work. They can't wait to get up in the morning and get started. They are eager and energetic. They are filled with purpose and totally committed to their mission. This kind of passion comes from loving and enjoying your work. It comes from doing what you were born to do. It comes from following your heart and trusting your joy as a guide. Enthusiasm and passion comes as a result of caring about what you do. If you love your work, if you enjoy it, you are already a success.

HOW TO DEVELOP PASSION?

How can you develop passion in the most important areas of your life?

Let's look at your career for a moment. That's the work that occupies the majority of your week. Ask yourself: Am I doing what I love to do?

If you aren't and you had the choice to do anything you wanted to do, what would that be? If you believe you can't make money doing that, imagine that you just won the lottery. After buying your expensive bungalow, a BMW and all the toys and travel you wanted, what would you do with your day? What you are doing now or something different?

The most successful people I have met are successful because they have found a way to make a living doing what they love to do.

Pay attention too, to those times outside of the office when you feel the happiest, the most joyous, the most fully engaged, the most acknowledged and appreciated, and the most connected with yourself and others. What were you doing at those times? What were you experiencing? Those events are indicators of ways you can bring passion into your life outside your day to day work. It tells you what you would be happiest doing with your time.

HOW TO KEEP PASSION AND ENTHUSIASM ALIVE?

Passion is a powerful tool for success and as such deserves to be an area you must consistently work on.

Passion makes your days fly by. It helps you get more done in less time. It helps you make better decisions. And it attracts others to you. They want to be associated with you and your success.

So how can you maintain passion and enthusiasm every day? The most obvious thing is to spend more time doing what you love to do. That includes discovering your true purpose, deciding what you really want to do and have, believing you can do and have it. Another key to passion and enthusiasm is to reconnect with you the original purpose for doing anything that you do.

When you express your passion and enthusiasm, you will become a magnet to others, who will be attracted to your high level of energy. They will want to play with you, work with you, and support your dreams and goals. As a result, you will ultimately get more done in a shorter period of time.

When you have passion and enthusiasm alive, it will never allow you to settle in your comfort zone. You will chart out your priorities; will be much happier feeding your passion with new things and by always being in the quest of taking it to the next level.

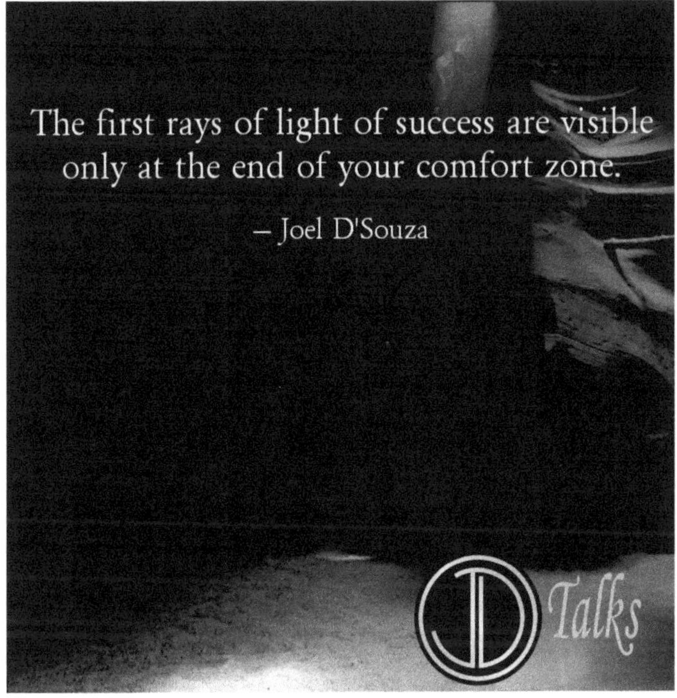

CHAPTER SEVEN

TRAIN YOUR INTUITION

During this period of time my daughter Joanne was born (my life's 5th defining moment) prematurely in just 6.5 month term in Mumbai. The doctors had to intervene the pregnancy to take control of my wife's deteriorating health. As one of Jehovah's Witnesses, we do not take blood, neither give. Our religious faith and trust in our God Jehovah was tested then when the doctors said that there was a high chance of death of both the mother and the child during the surgery process. I was emphatically told if our child survives, it would be abnormal or mentally retarded. The head nurse insisted that we accept blood. She even touched my wife's emotional chords showing her my son who was just 1 year and 9 months old. Despite the pressure, I remained calm and I said I will respect my wife's wishes. It is her decision. My wife too remained firm.

Once my wife confirmed her decision, I stepped in and suggested the alternatives to the doctors. My curiosity for learning and knowledge had made me study the alternatives available and I was able to suggest the doctors the alternatives. I had to make the biggest decision of my life!

My wife or my second child! Lose one of them or both! Gladly the trust in my God Jehovah had developed my intuition and I went by it. We remained firm in our decision and told the doctors we would accept whatever that would happen. During this critical surgery, when all my family was in a panic mode and extremely stressed, I was very calm. My extraordinary calmness surprised my father-in-law. This calmness in me was indeed a divine gesture of God.

My daughter Joanne was born, a tiny beauty, and immediately admitted to the Neonatal ICU. My wife and my daughter both survived the crisis and our trust in our God was rewarded. Within 48 hours of Joanne's birth, she had to undergo a major surgery on her stomach abnormality and we were given 96 hours as critical period post-surgery for her to survive. She being a little fighter that she was survived this critical phase. After about 45 days in the Neonatal ICU, we brought our tiny beauty home. My friends and family were a great help during this time since we needed a lot of money and moral support. My father and my friend Aju Oommenn helped me with money and my boss Tushar Mehta and my team made sure that my absence was not felt in my work place as they made up for it. My daughter had no complications whatsoever further in life. She is a very intelligent and beautiful child with a sharp mind. So much so for what the doctors told me before her birth! My intuition based on my strong belief system of my trust in Jehovah our God paid rich dividends! My knowledge of blood transfusion alternatives served me better when a few months later my mother-in-law was diagnosed with a serious liver ailment and her blood count had dropped drastically. I was able to convince the doctors about the alternatives of blood transfusion and in a few days my mother-in-law was hale and hearty.

TRUST YOUR INTUITION

For most of us, our education system and parenting system was always focused on looking outside of ourselves for the answers to our questions. Few of us have had any training on how to look inside, and yet most of the super-successful people have developed their intuition and learned to trust their gut feelings and follow their inner guidance. Many practice some form of daily meditation to access this voice within. This voice is trained according to what your belief system is.

HOW YOUR INTUITION COMMUNICATES WITH YOU

Your intuition can communicate with you in many ways. You may get a message from within as a vision or a visual image while you are meditating or dreaming. I often get images while I am lying in bed after I first wake up, while I am meditating or taking a shower. It can come in a flash out of the blue or it can be a long, unfolding image like a movie.

Your intuition may speak to you as a hunch, a thought, or a voice actually telling you yes, no, go for it, or not yet. It might come as one resounding word, a short sentence, or a complete lecture. You may find you can dialogue with the voice for clarification or more information.

You may also receive a message from your intuition through your physical senses. If the message is one of watch out or be careful, you may experience it as a chill, the creeps, a sense of restlessness, discomfort in your gut, constriction in your chest, tightness or pain in your head, even a sour taste in your mouth. A positive or yes message might come in the form of goose bumps, a dizzy feeling, warmth, a sense of opening or expansiveness in the chest, a sense of relaxation, a feeling of relief, or a letting go of tension.

You may also experience intuitive message through your emotions, such as a feeling of uneasiness, concern or confusion. Or when information is of a positive nature, you may experience a feeling of joy, euphoria, or profound inner peace.

Sometimes it is just a sense of knowing. How many times have you heard someone say “I don’t know, how I knew, I just knew” or “I knew it in my heart” or “in the depth of my soul”?

An indicator that the message is truly from your intuition is that it will often be accompanied by a sense of greater clarity, a feeling of rightness about the answer or the impulse.

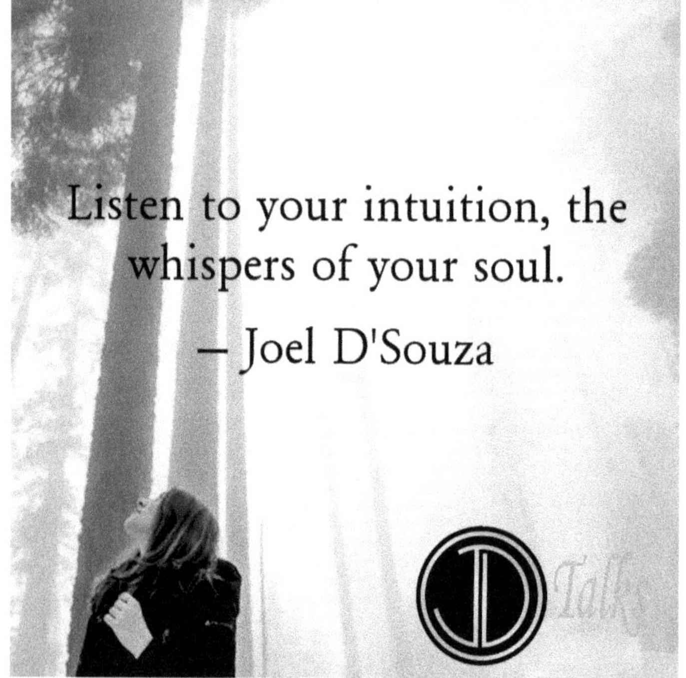
Listen to your intuition, the
whispers of your soul.
– Joel D'Souza
Talks

CHAPTER EIGHT

USE FAILURES TO STEP UP YOUR WAY TO SUCCESS

What happens when you give in to the routine of our lives? What happens when you allow your past failures and insecurities to decide your future?

You become trapped and blocked in your minds.You don't get trapped on purpose, it just happens. You get surrounded by people who are mediocre, incompetent, don't support your ambitions, actively oppose your ideas, make you feel guilty about your achievements, passion & dreams. It results in same stagnant jobs & relationships making you stuck in the whirlpool of life and you start taking irrational decisions causing you irreparable damages. Your repeated failures take you to a state where you don't visualize yourselves happy and negativity creeps in.

I resumed work, happy to be with my complete family. Life seemed sorted.

But the daily grinds of raising 2 small kids caught up with us. Rising expenses were not in sync with my income. The challenge to handle our kids as they grew up was sometimes too much. It resulted in fights between me and my wife. High tempers became too common.

I was again promoted 2 levels because of my performance and my relentless growth in my company brought along with it the insecurities of others. After my boss quit for better opportunities, the dirty corporate politics started to show up against me and that dejected me. My reputation in my religious organization was questioned by some senior members and my impeccable track record in my religious congregation life was blotted. I was not given my due of a senior responsibility in our religious congregation. This was my life's 6th defining moment. We were coded in our lives to think that senior responsibilities in our religious congregation were everything. My father especially drilled in me the thought that senior responsibilities in our religious congregation were the highest priority in our lives. And so when I was ignored for a privilege that was rightfully mine, I sulked. The sustained pain of ignorance that I endured over a long period of time became too much to handle. I was coded to think from childhood that such ignorance meant that I was worthless. These feelings of worthlessness and increasing stress resulted in frequent fights with my wife. I was in tremendous stress which contributed to a skin related sickness that I got afflicted with for almost 2 years. All kinds and forms of expensive treatments were tried, but to no relief. Finally, a 4th doctor I consulted put me on steroid based medicines which healed the sickness, but in turn made me pile on a lot of weight.

When one is in a bad state of mind, the decisions taken during those times have a permanent impact on their lives.

Making irrational decisions takes center stage all the while justifying it and living in denial about its success or failure. Here are the things that I did:

- I quit my job and decided to start something of my own. I just couldn't take that corporate nonsense anymore and didn't want to see the faces of the clowns in my office. I was done with them. Though I made some great friends for life during the five years I spent in the company, the worst ones also were there itself!
- I joined hands with a young entrepreneur and spent the next 1 year working with him developing a few software programs. During this period I had no income and I borrowed money from one of my friends to invest in my new venture. Unfortunately my frequencies with the young entrepreneur didn't match and we parted ways.
- The emotional fool that I was, to help a friend in need, I setup a small business for him in a suburb near Mumbai. He was not experienced in his skill to do that business but my emotional connect with him made me help him. That business tanked in 6 months and I lost all my money invested in it.
- I was under immense pressure now. I sold my house, paid off the loan onto it and with the remaining money, bought another 2 BHK house a little far off from the city but with more amenities than the previous house.
- I joined hands with another good friend of mine; we shared ideas of new concepts and started working on it. We had no income all along; on the contrary we had expenses to keep the company floating. We did it together for almost 2 years before I drained all my

savings and became a pauper with a debt of 2 million rupees!

I was a complete failure, destined to doom by my own acts! My cumulative losses in the distress house sale, no income for 3 years, spending all my savings were more than 6 million rupees!

As a result of all the accumulated stress, the fights at home were at its peak. I do not blame my wife for it since I was responsible for the mess that I made. She sacrificed her career for the kids, she had to give up her dream house, and she was left alone to fend for the kids while I was trying to build a business. Her anger on me and her reactions were completely justified.

At one point it became so unbearable that I walked out of the house in an attempt to end my life. I called my sister, cried my heart out loudly on the phone, disconnected it and went on my way to call it quits. At that time an unexpected call came on my phone. That call was of my partner Samson who was more than a dear friend. I answered that call and he knew from my voice something was drastically wrong. He convinced me come to office and I did just that. I spoke about my problem to him and he understood me. He took a commitment from me that I will never try to end my life again and that nothing is lost. A life time is there to put things in order. I agreed to work on the options he gave. The writing was clear on the wall now. I had neither the experience nor the skills to run a business. I was employed for 18 years before I switched to entrepreneurship with no knowledge of it. I still had an employee mindset rather than an employer mindset. I was simply incapable to handle any kind of business! This was my life's 7th defining moment.

Why we make irrational decisions?

All human decisions are made with emotions, at least in part. Anything that doesn't have a clear and precise outcome requires that we use our emotions in order to fill in the gaps. That means, that every decision we make, to some degree, is based on more than just being rational. Human decision making requires emotions. Our brains are coded such that we think everything we do makes perfect, logical sense. The decisions each of us makes are based on our understanding of the complex structure of morality and culture, combined with our past experience. We don't make decisions based on numbers and data (although we often think we do). We are taking our collective experience and feelings about those experiences, our understanding of the rules in which we are living or working, and the points of view of those around us who have authority - then making a decision based on all of this background.

Often when you make a decision it doesn't make sense to others, it's because you lack key information. It doesn't make sense to them, because they know that information. You may not have that information because you didn't know it was available, did not understand its importance, or you didn't have the experience or competence to know to ask for that information. You lack the skills to be able to make a different decision. Sometimes, bad decisions are based not on limited knowledge, but limited capability. Have you heard the expression, *"If the only tool you have is a hammer, every problem is a nail?"* When at work, you have a different tool set of how to tackle the various tasks and situations that you are faced with. If someone only has one or two tools that they are able to use, using that tool is the only thing they can do.

Unfortunately, all too often, it's difficult to admit a

deficiency in abilities. Rather than admit that we don't know how to do something, we work around it as best as we can, then defend our work around. This defense of our work around, can lead to even more irrational behavior in order to make sense of our previous decisions. You need to be aware of your own emotions and those of others, and if appropriate, acknowledge them. Often, putting a supportive spotlight on the fact that you are using emotions to reach a decision can help you see how they are affecting you or others in a negative way.

You need to educate and train yourselves. When you are making a decision, check to see if you have enough knowledge, training or education to make a good decision. If you don't, there will be a gap in competency.

Accepting that irrational decisions will be made by you or others because you are humans and not robots is an important step to being a successful person. Managing these situations can be tricky, but with the right approach, you can learn better about yourselves as well and those you are working with.

This is how you learn from your failed experiences, make a course correction and take a corrected leap forward.

If you fail, never think of bouncing back.
Learn from the failure and focus on BOUNCING FORWARD.
– Joel D'Souza
JD Talks

CHAPTER NINE

ACKNOWLEDGE YOUR POSITIVE PAST

Most people in our culture remember their failure more that their successes.

When you were a young child, your parents left you alone when you were playing and being cooperative, and then zapped you when you made too much noise, were a nuisance, or got into trouble.

Because the brain more easily remembers events that were accompanied by strong emotions, most people underestimate and under appreciate the number of successes they have had in relation to the number of failures they have had. One of the ways to counteract this phenomenon is to consciously focus on and celebrate your successes.

The sad truth is that we all have many more victories than failures – it is just that we set the bar too high for what we call a success.

Research has shown over and over again that the more you acknowledge your past successes, the most confident you become in taking on and successfully accomplishing new ones. You know that even if you fail, it won't destroy you because your self-esteem is high, and the more you take risks, the more you win in life. The more shots you take the more chances you have of scoring.

Whenever you complete anything successfully, write it down as a victory log. Start your own victory log as soon as possible, if you want, you can also embellish it like a scrapbook with photos, certificates, memos, and other reminders of your success.

DISPLAY YOUR SUCCESS SYMBOLS

Researchers have discovered that what you see in your environment has a psychological impact on your moods, your attitudes, and your behavior. Your environment has a great deal of influence over you. But here's an even more important fact - you have almost total control over your immediate environment. You get to choose what pictures are hung on your bedroom or office wall, what memorabilia get taped to your refrigerator or locker door, and what mementos you place on your desk or in your cubicle at work.

A valuable technique that will help build your self-esteem and motivate you to greater future success is the practice of surrounding yourself with awards, pictures and other objects that remind you of your successes.

Make a special place - a special shelf, the top of your dressing table, the refrigerator door, a victory wall in a hallway you pass through every day - and fill it with your success symbols.

We are not trained to acknowledge ourselves. In fact, we are mostly trained to do the opposite: Don't blow your own horn. Don't get a swelled head. Pride is a sin. As you begin to act more positive and nurturing toward yourself, it is natural to have physical and emotional reactions as you release the old negative parental wounds, unrealistic expectations, and self-judgments. If you experience any of these things - and not all people do - don't let these things stop you. They are only temporary and will pass after a few days.

REWARD YOUR INNER CHILD WITH A SENSE OF COMPLETION

Another reason to celebrate your successes is that you don't feel complete until you have been acknowledged or recognized. It gives you a sense of accomplishment and recognition. If you spend weeks producing a critical report and your boss doesn't acknowledge it, you feel incomplete. If you send someone a gift and get no acknowledgment, there's this little incomplete taking up attention units inside of you. Your mind needs to complete the cycle.

Even more important that completing, the simple, enjoyable act of acknowledging and rewarding our successes causes our subconscious mind to say *Hey succeeding is cool. Every time we produce a success, we get to do something that is fun.*

Rewarding yourself for your wins powerfully reinforces your subconscious mind.

For a few months my son was suffering from repeated stomach infections. He was hospitalized twice and the experience made him dreadful to even look at doctors or nurses. During the second hospitalization, after the treatment course, when his problem was still not getting better we sent his reports to a senior pediatric surgeon in Mumbai. He asked me to shift my son to a reputed hospital in Mumbai. I did so, and within 2 days my son was fit and fine to go home! The doctor advised me to stay for 2 weeks in Mumbai just in case the problem with him relapses. I stayed with my parents in Kalyan, a suburb near Mumbai for those 15 days. My son's stomach problem didn't relapse.

During those 15 days, I had nothing to do. Out of boredom one day I took my brother Allen's car for service at the company authorized service center. Next day I took my sister Benita's car for service at a prominent road side garage. At both places I acted ignorant as a commoner who had no knowledge about cars and let them do what they wanted with the cars. I paid those huge bills for no work done. My experiences at both these places were miserable and I found out that everyone in this industry cheats!

That is when I thought that something should be done about this. I wanted to give people full value of their money spent on car service and repairs, educate them on basic preventive maintenance tips and make sure they don't get cheated anymore. I went around the area where my parents stayed and figured out that there were huge numbers of cars in the vicinity. My passion and my childhood dream kick started.

Here I was with a 2 million rupees debt, having lost more than 6 million rupees, 3 recent failed businesses, not sure about the future and a family to take care of!

But I didn't want to dwell on my failures! I knew my knowledge base built over from my childhood will not defeat me. This is what I always wanted to do. I could do it. My positive affirmations kicked my soul and said "get going mate, you can do it." My intuition supported my dream and the concept that was running in my mind since childhood started to take shape. After coming back to Pune and I put the concept on paper. I quickly thought of a business name, registered a domain and made my own website on which

I put down my concept creatively. When I discussed this plan with my family, everyone was up in arms against me saying car garage is our not our forte, it is a dirty job and so on. Everyone around discouraged me saying the concept will fail, but I backed myself and asked a few of my friends to invest money.

Whoa – borrowing more money when already in a huge debt! My friends knew me and my passion for cars very well and they backed me up and funded my idea as investors. They didn't lend me money. They invested in my concept. I zeroed on to a rental place close to my parents' house in Kalyan near Mumbai. I was so excited that my dream venture was taking shape and during the course of the setup got some business associates who supported me and tied up with me to provide value added services, and so EXPRESS AUTOCARE was born on 1st August 2015, a multi brand car maintenance and detailing center which would eventually be a game changer. Since the entire focus was providing honest services, I put up high definition cameras in each service bay to give real time camera feed to clients on their smart phones to see what is happening with their cars. They could zoom and see what exactly is happening with their cars and were free to call us to give them a parallel update as they see their cars being worked upon on their phones. I made a customer lounge in my setup for clients to sit and see what is happening with their car. I hired some of the best technicians, got the latest equipment and machinery and each technician was trained to talk and educate clients on car maintenance tips. I worked along with my technicians and was thoroughly enjoying it. We made different service packages tailored to suit each class and brand of car. The focus was on giving the highest degree of satisfying customer experience.

I completely exited from the software company which was still operational though in losses and moved to stay with my parents in Kalyan. Since my kids' academic year had already started, my wife and kids stayed back in Pune. I used to visit them once a week, often riding my motorcycle all the way to Pune, a distance of about 180 kilometers to save money on travel.

EXPRESS AUTOCARE settled down, got great accolades, slowly built its customers database and we were reputed in the market. We just started to break even. What started as my childhood passion and dream, I lived through bad times, seized the opportunity and converted my dream to reality.

We are well trained to attach strong negative emotions to our mistakes and failures. Fact is that we succeed more than we fail. But we have kept the benchmark of success very high. Celebrate your every small victories and see how brave you become and how easy life becomes!

– Joel D'Souza

CHAPTER TEN

USE FEEDBACK TO BUILD

Feedback is the breakfast of champions.

- ***Ken Blanchard***

There are two kinds of feedback you might encounter - negative and positive. We tend to prefer the positive - that is, result, money, praise, a raise, a promotion, satisfied customers, awards, happiness, inner peace, intimacy, pleasure. It feels better. It tells us that we are on course that we are doing the right thing.

We tend not to like negative feedback - lack of results, little or no money, criticism, poor evaluations, being passed over for a raise or a promotion, complaints, unhappiness, inner conflict, loneliness, pain. However, there is as much useful data in negative feedback as there is in positive feedback. It tells us that we are off course, headed in the wrong direction, doing the wrong thing. That is also valuable information.

Treat negative feedback as information about "improvement opportunities."

Giving up and quitting - How many times have you or someone you know received negative feedback and simply gave up over it? All that does is keep you stuck in the same place.

Getting mad at the source of the feedback - Think about it. How many times have you reacted with anger and hostility towards someone who was giving you feedback that was genuinely useful? All it does is push the person and the feedback away. Imagine you are actually letting go a person who can help you improve.

Ignoring the feedback - Not listening to or ignoring the feedback is another response that doesn't work. We all know people who mute out everyone's point of view and blow their own. They are simply not interested in what other people think. They don't want to hear anything anyone else has to say. The sad thing is feedback could significantly transform their lives, if only they would only *listen*.

Crying and falling apart is simply ineffective. It may temporarily release whatever emotions you have built up in your system, but it takes you out of the game. It doesn't get you anywhere. It simply immobilizes you. It is not a great success strategy. Succumbing and giving up doesn't work either. It may make you feel safer and may stop the flow of negative feedback but it doesn't get you the good stuff. You can't win in the game of life if you are not on the playing field.

Getting angry at the person giving you the feedback is equally ineffective. It just makes the source of the valuable feedback attack you back or simply go away. What good is that? It may temporarily make you feel better, but it doesn't help you get more successful.

Remember feedback is simply information. You don't have to take it personally. Just welcome it and use it. The most intelligent and productive response is to say "Thank you for the feedback. Thank you for caring enough to take the time to tell me what you see and how you feel. I appreciate it".

Ask for your feedback!

Most people will not voluntarily give you feedback. They are as uncomfortable with possible confrontation as you are. They don't want to hurt your feelings. They are afraid of your reaction. They don't want to risk your disapproval. So to get honest and open feedback, you are going to need to ask for it... and make it safe for the person to give it to you. In other words don't shoot the messenger.

Be willing to ask.

My customers could see my passion clearly. But what I asked from them is a feedback of our services. The concept I built was new and we were executing it when there was no evidence of success. Customer feedback became the key to learn and improvise. Though many customers gave positive feedbacks, I was more interested on getting negative ones. I firmly believe negative feedback is a kind of constructive criticism. It is criticism that helps us to construct something better. I asked for more and more sincere feedback and I go it. By doing this, I was also building great relationships with them. With all the feedbacks, we improvised. We became quite reputed in the city with some honest customer reviews on social media platforms and word of mouth publicity. In no time the cream crowds of the city were all our customers who included top doctors, lawyers, police officers, municipal officers and prominent businessmen. We started getting our clients from as far as 200 kilometers. Within a year of starting we launched our own mobile app. Before the start of next academic year I rented out a 1 BHK flat and moved my family here in Kalyan. My wife and kids had no choice but to adjust with me in a 1 BHK apartment with not even basic amenities like a lift in the building. My kids often cursed me for giving them these downgrades!

But imagine on the other side, I was living through my dream in reality! While living in my dream, I completely got over the worthlessness I felt when rejected for a privilege in my religious congregation. It didn't matter to me anymore since it was actually a blessing in disguise. I was no longer a part of the race to the top in my religious congregation. It gave me a lot more freedom in my thinking and time to pursue things I always wanted to do. I learnt to rely more on my God than the people around. I realized I was coded for wrong priorities all along. My priorities in my life were well defined now.

All these experiences coded my mind to believe what I had learnt in school "Whatever happens, happens for the best!" The 25 rupees that I didn't get from my mother eventually made me attain my dream and live through it!

TRANSCEND YOUR LIMITING BELIEFS

Your subconscious mind does not argue with you. It accepts what your conscious mind decrees. If you say "I can't afford it", your subconscious mind works to make it true. Select a better thought. Say "I will buy it. I accept it in my mind".

Many of us have beliefs that limit our success - whether they are beliefs about our own capabilities, beliefs about what it takes to succeed, beliefs about how we should relate with other people, or even common myths that modern day science or studies have long since refuted.

Moving beyond your limiting beliefs is a critical first step toward becoming successful.

You can learn how to identify those beliefs that are limiting you and then replace them with positive ones that support your success.

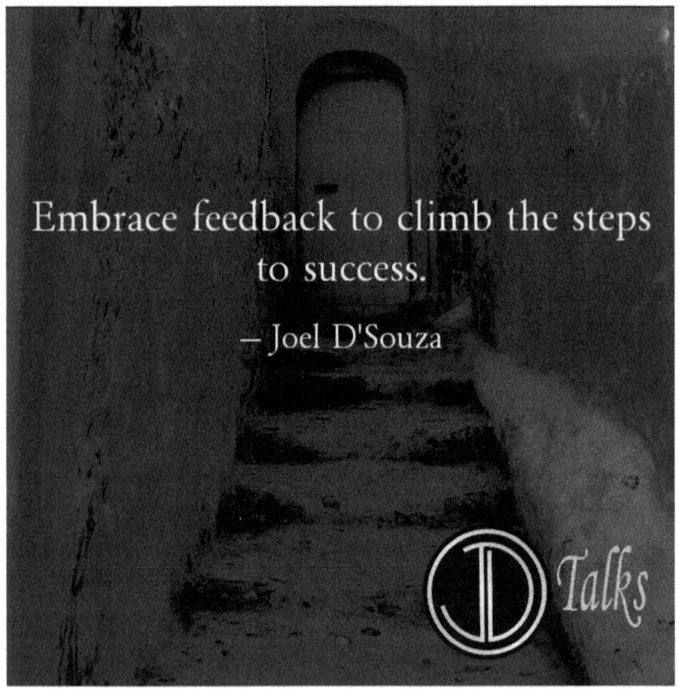

CHAPTER ELEVEN

EMBRACE CHANGE

Change is the law of life. And those who look only to the past or present are certain to miss the future. What works today may not work tomorrow.

Change is inevitable.

At this very moment, for instance, your body and cells are changing. The earth is changing. The economy, technology, how we do business, even how we communicate is changing. And though you can resist that change and potentially be swept by it, you can also choose to cooperate with it, adapt to it and benefit from it.

WHERE DO YOU NEED TO GROW?

When change happens, you can both cooperate with it and learn how to benefit from it or you can resist it and eventually get run over by it. It's your choice.

When you embrace change wholeheartedly as an inevitable part of life, looking for ways to use new changes to make your life richer, easier and more fulfilling, your life will work much better. You will experience change as an opportunity for growth and new experience.

HOW TO EMBRACE CHANGE

Realize that there are two kinds of change - ***cyclical change and structural change*** - neither of which you can control.

Cyclical change such as the change we see in the stock markets happens several times a year.

We see seasonal change in the weather, holiday spending by the public, more travel in the summer, and so on. These are changes that happen in cycles, and frankly we just accept as a normal part of life.

But there are also structural changes - such as when the computer was invented and completely changed how we live, work, get our news and make purchases. When smart phones came, things changed radically. More recently Artificial Intelligence has arrived to sweep people off their feet. Structural changes are the kinds of changes where there is no getting back to doing things the way they were before. And these are the kinds of changes that can sweep you away if you resist them.

Remember back of a time when you experienced a change but resisted. Perhaps it was a move, a job transfer, a change in suppliers, a change in technology in your company, a change in management, or even your teenager going off to college - a change you were going to have to deal with and you thought it was the worst thing in the world.

What happened once you surrendered to the change? Did your life actually eventually improve? Can you look back now and say, "Wow I am glad that happened. Look at the good it eventually brought me!"

If you can always remember that you have been through changes in the past and that they have largely worked out for the best - you can begin to approach each new change with the excitement and anticipation you should.

Just as EXPRESS AUTOCARE started to break even, we encountered a structural change that the entire country went through – the challenge of demonetization. The high value running currency of Rs. 500 and Rs. 1,000 was rendered as worthless by the government in India. The market drastically slowed down. Economy was in doldrums. Customers stopped coming and we were not even able to cover our running costs. After a month it got me extremely worried as I didn't have money to pay my staff salaries, pay my suppliers or even to cover the basic utility bills. In such a situation, a customer walked in and read the worries on my face. He asked me the problem and I told him the reality. He was surprised and I knew at this rate I will have to close down the business by the following month. I was distraught! The customer walked out and came back in 5 minutes and volunteered to invest money in EXPRESS AUTOCARE so that we would survive this challenging phase. He just said, "I do not want EXPRESS AUTOCARE to run out of breath while facing such challenges". A customer who serviced his car just once with us had that level of confidence in our honest business model. That level of confidence of clients in our honest business model was just what we needed to boost our morale. I did not take his money. I convinced my wife and my mother to hand over all their gold to me. I pledged their gold and raised money to keep us running. The landlords of my business place were gracious enough to reduce the rent. It further boosted our confidence and we worked harder. We innovated our work processes further and our business associates too co-operated with us. We added more and more value added services. I got the pledged gold of my wife and mom out in 6 months. We were back to break even!

Did I say I spoke too early? Well, just as EXRPRESS AUTOCARE found its wheels back, a new structural change swept the entire country - government mandate of GST (Goods & Service Tax) hit us very badly. Though the concept was great and it was the need of the hour, its implementation was not well planned. The market grinded to a halt as the entire supply chain got affected. All my clients got busy with its implementation for their businesses and car repairs or service was the last thing in their minds. Also since the supply chain was affected, sourcing spare parts became extremely difficult. Once again we were sailing in the same boat as we were about 7-8 months back.

I was extremely disappointed. I had no choice but to raise funds again and I again pledged the same gold which I released a month ago. That money sufficed us for 2 months but the market didn't recover in that time. It took more than 5 months for the market to revive. Meanwhile, the question was whether to continue the business or put this in the failed business basket of mine! The past evidence of business recovering and coming to break even gave me the courage to go to my bank and ask an overdraft facility on my business account. After the necessary paperwork, the bank sanctioned the overdraft amount. We got a breath of life and managed to keep our heads above the water. Over a period of time, I realized that the structural change that the government did that of introducing GST worked well for me. I reduced my burden of different taxations and I was able to avail government schemes because of my compliance to it. But there was a greater realization too. I realized that market conditions may change anytime and every time we cannot raise funds. I was doing something wrong in my business and I wasn't able to figure out what.

We were stagnant at one level and not growing.

Meanwhile, I sold my 2 BHK apartment in Pune and bought a 1 BHK apartment in the same building where we were staying on rent. The resistance from the entire family was very high for a 1 BHK flat. But we had stayed now for 2 years in a rented 1 BHK apartment, so it was easy for my wife and kids to accept it.

I was able to clear a large part of my debts after selling the apartment in Pune. I had to take small housing loan to buy this 1 BHK apartment in Kalyan. We did up the interiors of the house and we as a family realized that we have all that we *need,* all the *wants* were got rid of. We learnt to be happy in our small world though for some time my wife and kids visited the past and cursed me for the huge lifestyle change I made them undergo. I accept it as a fact of life, ignore it and just move on.

SAY NO TO THE GOOD SO THAT YOU CAN SAY YES TO THE GREAT.

GOOD IS THE ENEMY OF GREAT.

What a simple concept it is, yet you would be surprised how frequently even the world's top entrepreneurs, professionals, educators, and civic leaders get caught up in projects, situations, and opportunities that are merely good, while the great is left out in the cold, waiting for them to make room in their lives.

THE PARETO PRINCIPLE - WHEN 20% EQUALS 80%

If you surveyed your life and jotted down those activities that brought you the most success, the most financial gain, the most advancement, and the most enjoyment, you would discover that about 20% of your activity produces about 80% of your success. This phenomenon is the basis for the Pareto Principle, named after the nineteenth century economist who discovered

80% of an enterprise's revenue comes from 20% of its customers.

HOW CAN YOU DETERMINE WHAT'S TRULY GREAT, SO YOU CAN SAY NO TO WHAT'S MERELY GOOD?

- Start by listing your opportunities - one side of the page for good and the other side for great.
- Talk to advisors about this potential new pursuit.
- Test the waters.
- And finally look at where you spend your time.

We, our people and our organizations are a bundle of mind-sets – *UNKNOWINGLY!*

Exponential growth in life and business & extra-ordinary results are not possible with the same mind-set. We need to be willing to embrace change to reach the next level. When we stop being a perfectionist or self-obsessed, we have a multiplier effect on ourselves. We must identify our distinct forte and work on it. Similarly we need to build distinct forte teams in our business. Hiring people who like creative challenges, who love to work in teams, who know that great rewards come from making valuable contribution to the growth of the organization, will eventually form a great team which is focused and aligned with the organization goals. When this happens you get your freedom to do:

- What you love to do and do best
- BWY (Be With Yourself) days
- Connect with opportunities, people who are exponential thinkers, resources that multiply your quality of life.

- Pursue your multiple interests and hobbies.

Yet another field where we need to constantly embrace change is the field of technology. We must love technology. Enterprises like Meta, Tesla, Zerodha, Zoho, Amazon, Flipkart, OLA, Uber, OYO Rooms, AirBNB, Zomato, Swiggy, etc. adopted technology for their exponential growth.

Technology will kill normal entrepreneurs who are not focused for exponential growth. Such entrepreneurs are like beginner drivers who try to drive a Ferrari. It will kill them.

Technology brings happiness to a renewed mindset. Technology means teamwork made automatic. Technology connects you to people, opportunity, money, resources anywhere in the world. It helps you to create solutions. There is nothing that technology cannot do.

For a normal entrepreneur, technology means

- Impossible demands
- Confusing
- Overwhelming
- Upsetting
- Regressive
- Disruptive

... resulting in being complaining, afraid and always in a rejection mode.

Whereas technology romances the exponential growth guys, for exponential growth guys, technology is a multiplier. For normal growth guys, technology is a subtractor.

One fine day, my brother asked me to attend a seminar of Santosh Nair, a reputed business coach in Mumbai. That seminar changed my mindset to a great extent. It gave me the answers as to why my business was stagnant. I attended all his subsequent seminars. I started picking up books, reading business patterns and success stories of people. I realized that I need to keep on learning to be in business. I started my learning diligently. I took seriously everything that I learnt and that changed my business and more so my mindset. I now started attending almost all the business seminars that were happening in the city. Each seminar opened my eyes as to how illiterate I was in the business world! And I realized the need for more and more 'learning'!

At this juncture of my life where I was a struggling entrepreneur, I realized that if I want to successful, I have to invest in learning. With no money in hand I approached my father-in-law and mother-in-law for help. They were surprised that I was asking money for learning at this age, but when I told them the reality, they gladly pitched in. With all the learning, my employee mindset now evolved to an entrepreneur mindset.

I realized as an entrepreneur I was trapped in self-employment. I was doing menial jobs that I should not have done at all. I was employed in my own business. I was trying to do everything myself thinking that it is saving me a lot of money by not employing people to do the same jobs. The mistake I did was I didn't factor the value of my time! That's the reason why things got stagnant, and my stress levels were high. There was no growth in my company.

In line with what I was now learning, I took some critical actions. I started hiring people and created a second line of leadership. I trained them with the help of various resources that were available with me. I invested more money and upgraded our mobile app with more features. I invested in an online billing and CRM system to automate billing and taxation. I trained my team on using the app and the billing system. Technology made our lives simpler. Eventually, the team and technology took over all my work. I stopped working *in* my business and started working *on* my business. I had enough time to think and change service processes and add more value to them. I came up with innovative ideas and forged more business relationships with associates. I started networking with people. I made friends with people from different business profiles. I joined professional networking forums from where business started flowing in. I learnt from them the tricks and trades of business. Every time I learnt something, I figured out how we can implement it in EXPRESS AUTOCARE. We tweaked our processes every now and then, resulting in better customer satisfaction each time. My turnover increased and customer retention rate peaked. My team now takes care of almost all the activities at EXPRESS AUTOCARE giving me sufficient time and freedom to work on my business.

As time went by, a new marketing technique swept the market – Digital Marketing. So new conditions called for different marketing techniques. I had to adapt. If I didn't lean into the change that was coming at me and instead tried to protect myself by continuing old ways of marketing my business, then I would have ended up being frozen in a mountain, so to say.

"It is not because things are difficult that we do not dare;
it is because we do not dare that things are difficult"
Philosopher Seneca

Anyone in business is in show business, and when we are at work, we are on stage. We need to perform and mesmerize the audience. No one cares if you are having a bad day. They just want to see the show that they have paid to see.

Competition is fiercer than ever before. Customers are less loyal. They want to experiment with someone / something new every time. Digital and social media has totally altered the way we work. In such situations, if one does not change and adapt to the market demands, it will be only a matter of time for your end.

I took up this challenge and started to work on my personal brand and my company brand. I was hesitant at the beginning to shoot my videos and promote them as I was on the bulkier side and I was concerned about how the audience would view me and my message. *Any time you try something new, it's going to feel weird.*

I was patient with the process of change as change is always the messiest in the middle. Problems are only problems when we make them problems. I got over the initial fear and started shooting promotional videos for EXPRESS AUTOCARE. I hired a digital marketing agency that edited these videos and ran campaigns on social media sites. In the first year of such marketing techniques, our business grew by 35%.

Meanwhile, I started to work on my health and reduced my weight and made myself more presentable in the videos. As a result of extensive localized social media campaigns, I became a known face in the city. People appreciated the value additions in my videos and started following me. Almost everywhere in the city, people who use social media know me. My personal branding helped my business immensely. *Always remember that initiative and hard work is the warm-up act for a headliner called success.*

Now EXPRESS AUTOCARE is a well- known and settled enterprise expanded 5 fold since its inception.

Embrace change wholeheartedly.

Keep on learning.

Take actions immediately.

Do not procrastinate.

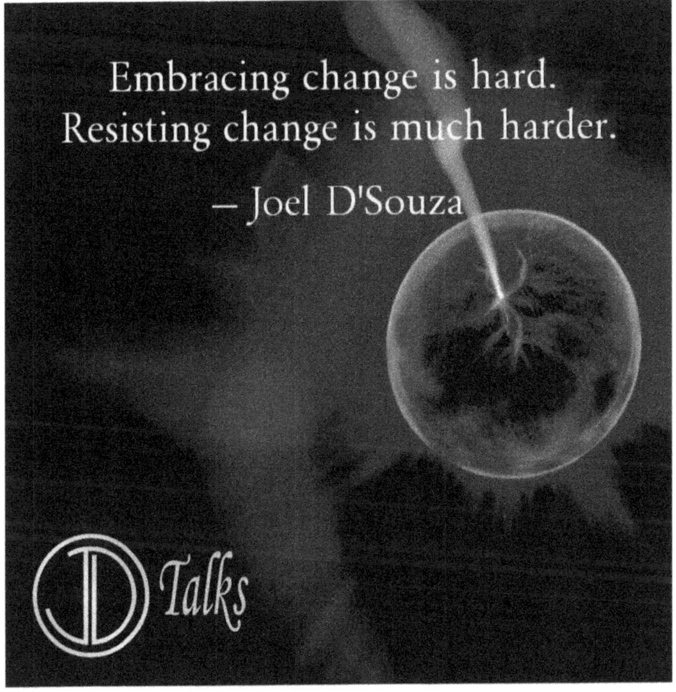

CHAPTER TWELVE

MASTERMIND YOUR WAY TO SUCCESS

Drop out of the "ISN'T IT AWFUL?" club... and surround yourself with successful people. Remember, you are the average of the five people you spend the most time with. If you want to be more successful, you have to start hanging out with more successful people. Pay any price to stay in the presence of extraordinary people. You need to be surrounded with those who have done it, you need to be surrounded with people who have a positive attitude and a solution oriented approach to life - people who know that they can accomplish whatever they set out to do. Confidence is contagious. So is lack of confidence.

There are two types of people - anchors and motors. Remove the anchors from your lives and get going with the motors because the motors are going somewhere and they are having more fun. The anchors will just drag you down. Be selective.Just do not hang around anybody that you don't want to be with. You can stay positive. Hang around with people who are happy, who are growing, who want to learn, who don't mind saying sorry or thank you and are having a fun time.

AVOID TOXIC PEOPLE

Until you reach the point in your self-development where you no longer allow people to affect you with their negativity, you need to avoid toxic people at all costs. Make a conscious effort to surround yourself with positive, nourishing, and uplifting people - people who believe in you, encourage you to go after your dreams, and applaud your victories. Surround yourself with possibility thinkers, idealists, and visionaries. You need to ask them to share their success strategies with you. Then try them on and see if they fit for you. Experiment with doing what they do, reading what they read, thinking the way they think, and so on. If the new ways of thinking and behaving work, adopt them. If not, drop them, and keep looking and experimenting.

When two or more people coordinate in a spirit of harmony and work toward a definite objective or purpose, they place themselves in position, through the alliance, to absorb power directly from the great storehouse of Infinite Intelligence.

We all know that two heads are better than one when it comes to solving a problem or creating a result. So imagine having a permanent group of five to six people who meet every week for the purpose of problem solving, brain storming, networking, and encouraging and motivating each other.

This process called Masterminding is one of the most powerful tools for success.

A PROCESS FOR ACCELERATING YOUR GROWTH

The basic philosophy of a mastermind group is that more can be achieved in less time when people work together. A mastermind group is made up of people who come together on a regular basis - weekly, biweekly or monthly to share ideas, thoughts, information, feedback, and resources. By getting the perspective, knowledge, experience, and resources of the others in the group, not only can you move beyond your own limited view of the world but you can also advance your own goals and projects more quickly.

But for a mastermind group to be powerfully effective, people must be comfortable enough with each other to tell the truth.

NEW THOUGHTS, NEW PEOPLE, NEW RESOURCES

When you form your mastermind group, consider bringing together people from different professional arenas and people that are above you and who can introduce you to a network of people you normally wouldn't have access to. Make the most of your mastermind group.

While I was working on my business growth, I created my mastermind circles and got rid of the toxic people from my life – be it family or friends, the toxic people were gone. I started giving out my knowledge and also getting knowledge through these mastermind circles. I got solutions for a few problems in my life and business and vice versa I started giving solutions for people with problems in their lives and businesses.

One fine day, one of my mastermind circle friend Datta Thorat who is a top of the table insurance agent called me at 1 PM on a Sunday and asked me if I can speak for an hour in their agents' forum at 3 PM, same day. At first I was worried as to how it would be possible with just 2 hours' notice but I was glad about the opportunity and I asked him the challenges they face in the insurance industry. He told me the challenges of the insurance industry. I did a brief study of it, prepared my material in that short time and delivered a power packed seminar for an hour addressing the issues they face and likely solutions. They asked me to talk for more time and I went on for another 2 hours. 3 hours of power packed seminar in front of a reputed insurance company agents was just the push I needed to try something different in my life. I realized that I can coach other people about what I learnt the hard way. This was the 8th defining moment of my life. I soon organized a ticketed seminar on Leveraging Business Growth through Technology, which was sponsored by a few friends in my mastermind circle. Attended by 25 people, it was received well by all. I got some valuable feedback from my mastermind circle friends to take the quality of my seminars to the next level. My freedom that I experienced in EXPRESS AUTOCARE allowed me start my yet another journey of being a Trainer, Speaker and Coach. I pursued professional life transformation and business growth coach training and got certified. I formed another company called IGNITING MINDS, a Business Training and Workshops company, where I became the Lead Trainer in Life and Business Coaching.

With no toxic people surrounding me who always belittled my dreams and ambitions and scoffed at me when I shared it with them, I reached my next level in life, thanks to my mastermind circle who recognized the spark in me and pushed me to go for it.

I also joined a local Rotary Club where I expanded my mastermind circle. Being with distinguished business owners, doctors, and other professionals in the cause of helping others, gave me a great sense of satisfaction. I kept learning from such ones, their business ideas, their struggles, their growth story and their giving back to the society inclination.

Another habit I established during this time is reading. Reading best sellers in the field of life and business and different aspects of it enhanced my cognitive abilities by promoting analytical thinking and expanding vocabulary. Reading also has emotional advantages, such as developing empathy and reducing stress levels. Moreover, it fosters social skills by improving communication, empathy, and appreciation for diverse cultures.

5 Benefits of Reading

- Reduces stress and helps you relax.
- Improves your concentration and memory.
- Vocabulary expansion and strengthens your writing abilities.
- Enhances your knowledge.
- Increases your imagination and creativity.

One book after another kept on expanding my mastermind circle. And till date I don't go to bed without reading for at least an hour.

Books are your best friends, so they say. It's indeed true!

High achievers surround themselves with other masterminds who challenge one another to keep improving, guide one another to greatness.

– Joel D'Souza

CHAPTER THIRTEEN

TURBULENT TIMES BUILD GREAT LEADERS

In October 2019, there was a fire incident in my office. At about 8 AM I received a call from a passerby (our workshop contact number is printed on our main signboard) that black fumes are coming out from the closed gate edges. I immediately rushed to the workshop and opened the main gate. To my shock, particularly my office was completely burnt down and the fire was about to spread outside the office. The passerby already had informed the fire brigade and within 10 minutes the fire brigade arrived and extinguished the fire. Thankfully nothing other than my office cabin was destroyed in the fire. Three cars, oil barrels etc. were in the workshop and had the fire spread, it would have been a disaster.

A leading Orthopedic Surgeon of the city, Dr. Prashant Sonawane, who was also our first customer, and who by then had become a good friend, was on his morning walk that day and he stopped by to check what had happened.

The moment he saw me, he understood how scared and shocked I was. I was literally trembling thinking how big this disaster would have been if not for the Good Samaritan passerby who called me and the fire brigade. Dr. Sonawane stood by me till the police and the fire officer arrived and gave us a report of the mishap for legal proceedings. He calmed my mind talking to me made sure my blood pressure was under control. He was with me for the next 4 hours till things settled down.

My friends also came, and were there with me till all legal formalities were completed. Two of my mastermind circle friends out of which one was Dr. Ashissh Jain came, and boosted my spirit saying how the damages were limited to my office only. They also told me that after the fire, as we throw the damaged things out, throw out all toxicity from your life, toxic relationships, friends and family members. I took this fire incident in my stride, dumped all toxic people from my life and next day we started our operations again. Yes, the very next day! None from my team sulked about the incident. We cleaned the area, removed damaged things and next day we started. All thanks to my friends, especially Dr. Ashissh Jain who made this possible.

As the news spread about the fire, many customers called to ensure our well-being, also committed financial help to pay for the damages and restart operations. I was overwhelmed with all the support received from friends and customers and realized that we at EXPRESS AUTOCARE really had touched people's lives.

Turbulent times made me realize about the value we had created so far in the city with our work. Also how I excelled as a leader whom my team looked up on, starting operations immediately with great determination. The fire was a result of a mistake of one of my team members, a woman employee. As the fire brigade informed us about the reason that caused the fire, it was evident who the culprit was from my team. Instead of creating a scene there, I handled the situation gracefully. Though she felt very guilty about what happened because of her negligence, I just made the team focus on the learning from the mishap and moved on. As I did not fire the team member, in our team meeting, myself and fellow team members boosted her morale and we pledged to me more careful in the future especially in safety measures. My handling of the situation in such a manner created a deep impact on my team and now they were more loyal and more committed as a team.

As mentioned in chapter 8 how certain situations make us take irrational decisions, my experiences and knowledge helped me to remain calm and take the right decisions. I had matured as a leader. The fire in my office and the subsequent quick recovery was the 9th defining moment of my life.

In January 2020 I had the opportunity to travel to Colombo, Sri Lanka to conduct a training program for entrepreneurs for 3 days. During this period I signed a yearlong calendar of training programs to be conducted in Sri Lanka with a local business associate Paul Navamani who was a good friend since my UAE days. I was pretty excited of the head start my training business IGNITING MINDS received.

But then the most turbulent period of this century so far, started in March 2020 and parts thereof of the same year. This period was the infamous "Covid Period" where the entire world came to a grinding halt, people being locked in their homes.

Many families were devastated by hospitalizations, loss of loved ones, loss of jobs, businesses closing down and economies getting destroyed. I also lost one of my best friends, Gills Baretto, who was more like an elder brother to me. He had helped me when I needed help the most. 27 years of friendship came to an abrupt end with his death. Lighting his pyre was the 10th defining moment of my life.

This period was a time life tested all of us. Such turbulent times also saw a lot of businesses unable to sustain and close down.

As with other business owners I too was extremely worried about the future, though very confident in our scientific and medical advancements that we will get over this soon. Being into a habit of reading helped a lot, I read a lot of books that I had and books on Amazon Kindle. In a way all this knowledge helped me in building my confidence to tackle life post the covid era.

But 2 months of shutdown, and subsequent small periods of shutdowns affected my business. A loss of a star team member in a road accident at such a time compounded our worries.

Because of uncertainty over government announcement of lockdowns, only businesses of essential supplies were operating and making some money. Rest all businesses actually had no business, sustaining the business even after lockdown was called off became a great challenge.

I approached my friend CA Tushar Jain to help me get a bank loan for working capital, and because of our good paper work and statutory compliances over the years, CA Tushar Jain got the loan sanctioned immediately and it helped us to find our feet back post the covid era.

EXPRESS AUTOCARE offered a lot of free and discounted services to car owners for some time after covid so that all got back on their feet without thinking much about money.

A smooth sea never made a skilled sailor
Franklin D. Roosevelt

Now was the test of leadership principles and qualities which I had read about and tried my best to implement the same.

During the entire covid period, my team was very worried about losing their jobs, salary reduction post covid and other issues. I conducted a team meeting on Zoom every week, asking about their well-being and assuring them their job security and being there for them in case anyone falls sick and contracts covid.

Just after the first lockdown was called off, when a star team member died of a road accident, the team keenly looked upon me as to how I handled the situation. Though it was not my official obligation, I helped in raising funds for his family and also sent his remains to Uttar Pradesh, 2,000 KMs away to his home town and family. My customers also appreciated this highly and they generously donated for his family. His son was only 17 days old when he died. After 2 months his entire family came all the way to meet me and thanked me for my support to them.

Once we started operations post covid, I personally called each of my team member to my office, assured each of them that they would not lose their jobs nor their salaries reduced. On the contrary I introduced an incentive system over and above the salary against slabs of our billing targets. This assured them of their jobs and they put more efforts in their work. Our workplace is leased and the landowner during the covid period had called me and assured me of no rent would be payable during non-productive periods of business. In fact he offered to pay back the rent which I paid after operations for a month post covid lock down.

The freebies and discounts that we offered to customers immediately post lockdown became a game changer. Customers became loyal to us, and more and more customers started referring us to others. The social media advertisement campaigns were well watched by people during lockdown and soon after lockdown our business soared to new heights. I had to hire more staff to cater to the demands. The space I had did not suffice me to handle the load of work. I optimized our processes, hired more team members, and got things done quickly reducing the turn-around time. Soon we became the talk of the town car workshop in the city.

Before covid, in 2019, my father suffered a heart attack post which his kidneys got damaged. From June 2019 to July 2023 (till he passed away), he was admitted to various hospitals a total of 37 times. From 2020 onwards he had to be put on hemodialysis for filtration of his kidneys. Thrice a week, for 30 months, his dialysis went on and in between many hospitalizations for his other ailments. He contracted covid twice in this period.

My father's sickness also kept us on toes every time and repeated hospitalizations and caring for him was truly challenging. My team and my friends were very helpful whenever needed to help us take care of my father. It was my mother's grit and determination for caring for my father; he survived despite all odds, eventually passing in July 2023. My mother was strength and determination personified. The way she managed my father for the last 4 years of his life despite her own frail health with an unwavering spirit displaying great resilience was worth admiring. I am also grateful to all the Doctors and fellow Rotarians, especially Rotarian Sanjay Machave for their support during such turbulent times.

During this time, just after the lock down in August 2020, with the enormous workload that we had, I had a severe bout of slipped disc with sciatica. The pain was so unbearable rendering me completely helpless in distress. I cried out to the doctor to cut my left leg as the pain was so immense! My blood pressure shot up so much because of the pain that the doctors put me in ICCU to monitor and control it. I was counseled by a doctor after my distress cries to cut off my left leg. After my hospitalization, for almost 1 month I was bed ridden. Further one month I was restrained at home undergoing physiotherapy.

My dear friend Anant Singh had lost his job during covid and he assured my wife that he will help run EXPRESS AUTOCARE with my team during my hospitalization and recovery period. He did a very good job in handling my business and he made me realize how well I had established systems and processes, how good and cooperative my team was and how easy it was for him to run the business operations even though he didn't have technical knowledge. I am extremely grateful to Anant for his efforts to keep my business running in my absence.

Sometimes we imagine turbulence in our minds. An upcoming structural change in automobiles is the influx of electric vehicles. Many are scared that this technology boom will take away a lot of jobs rendering many car service centers closed. Despite a lot of resistance, Electric Vehicles are the future.

How turbulent is it going to be for our business? Well, this threat is a just a perception. Every new technology brings with it a new set of jobs. I keep on telling my technicians that they will be out of jobs if they don't show a learning inclination and upgrade themselves. As a leader, I am preparing them for this upcoming technology disruption.

Recently to expand EXPRESS AUTOCARE we acquired another place which is huge and can cater up to 50 cars at a time. This place serves as an extension to our existing setup. We acquired the most advanced tools and machineries for this new workshop. This was my original dream. As a picture of mine was being clicked in the new setup, I for the first time felt proud of myself. I survived despite all odds.

My 16 year old son Leander, an equal car freak as I am, is well versed with most modern car technologies and its service methodologies. He uses his mobile phone to gather as much knowledge as possible and often works with technicians in EXPRESS AUTOCARE. I am nurturing his passion in cars, and preparing my succession plan. My son will take over my business after he completes his education and a mandatory 2 year work for some company stint.

EXPRESS AUTOCARE is future ready, no matter what disruptions may come.

Recently Maxson Lewis, Founder & CEO of Magenta Mobility (A Disruptive Enterprise in the EV Domain) invited me for a podcast in the studio of their office. This unscripted discussion was largely on automobile technology in India and about Electric Vehicles. During the one take shoot, I realized the depth of my knowledge in the automotive domain as I answered the questions put forth by Maxson. This podcast went viral on social media sites and on Linkedin. Since then, many business owners and prominent venture capitalists in the car service and EV domain have either called me to be on their advisory panel or to be associated with EXPRESS AUTOCARE.

With another exciting development recently, I came onboard a company called WOW AUTOLINK (Online Car

Service & Road Side Assistance Aggregator Company) as a Mentor and together with the core team, we re-branded it to MY FNG – Your Friendly Neighbourhood Garage.

I am now the Co-Founder and Chief Operations Officer (COO) of this rebranded company – MY FNG.

MY FNG is a network of carefully assessed and empaneled multi-brand car service centers who believe in honest & quality work, fair pricing, transparency and above all Customer Delight. With my expertise in this field, all the success formulas implemented and evolved with time at EXPRESS AUTOCARE is now available with MY FNG Service Partners.

With a goal to reach all cities in India soon, MY FNG intends to change the game of multi-brand car service centers by helping them grow their business, optimize their operations, enhance technical & soft skills and help enable digitization & branding, the right way – with systems, tools and processes.

I am excited to the core, as apart from being a mentor for the company, I am leading the Operations & Training teams of MY FNG with a very critical role to get on the ground and hand hold our service partners to success with integrity replicating the EXPRESS AUTOCARE model.

While many online car service aggregators came and went bankrupt and some are still burning investors' cash, MY FNG is here to stay and succeed with a 'heart on the sleeve' business model.

When I started EXPRESS AUTOCARE 9 years ago, I never thought that we would eventually endeavor to take the same business model across the country with a dynamic team at MY FNG. As I lead this journey to ensure highest customer delight with quality work and fair pricing in the car service and maintenance industry together with

Team MY FNG, we will achieve what no one else has - with systems & processes together with honesty & integrity.

As a leader, you need to be abreast with market conditions, need to continuously study and evaluate your domain developments, the economy, your country's political stability and so on. Only a voracious reader can be a great leader.

How to implement your learning in your business and help it grow asserts your leadership authority.

How you respond to turbulent times can make you a great leader or break you as helpless ordinary man.

After such turbulent times I realized –

- *Toxicity has no place in a happy life.*
- *The bigger the risks, the larger the rewards are.*
- *Things often have to fall apart before they can be rebuilt in a much better way.*
- *Normal is gone. Business unusual is the new usual.*
- *Complacency is the primary enemy of success and victory.*
- *The safest, most intelligent place to be out there is on the edge of that cliff always.*
- *Leadership shows and establishes itself only in turbulent times.*
- *As a leader you need to establish systems and processes to build your business.*
- *Your team decides the trajectory of your business. As a leader you need to be damn good to lead this trajectory positively.*
- *Your family is of primary importance, your top-most priority.*
- *You need meaningful friends all your life.*
- *You need to spend time with yourself often.*

What a beautiful thing it is to be able
to stand tall and say
"I fell apart, and I survived"

– Joel D'Souza

CHAPTER FOURTEEN

SEE WHAT YOU WANT & GET IT

Imagination is everything.
It is the preview of life's coming attractions.
– Albert Einstein

Visualization or manifestation – or act of creating compelling and vivid pictures in your mind – may be the most underutilized success tool you possess because it greatly accelerates the achievement of any success in three powerful ways.

- Visualization activates the creative powers of your subconscious mind.
- Visualization focuses your brain by programming its Reticular Activating System (RAS) to notice available resources that were always there but were previously unnoticed.
- Visualization magnetizes and attracts to you the people, resources, and opportunities you need to achieve your

goal.

Harvard University researchers found that students who visualized in advance performed tasks with nearly 100% accuracy, whereas students who didn't visualize achieved only 55% accuracy.

HOW VISUALIZATION WORKS TO ENHANCE PERFORMANCE

When you visualize your goals as already complete each and every day, it creates a conflict in your subconscious mind between what you are visualizing and what you currently have. Your subconscious mind tries to resolve that conflict by turning your current reality into the new more exciting vision.

This conflict when intensified over time through constant visualization, actually causes three things to happen:

- It programs your brain's RAS to start letting into your awareness anything that will help you achieve your goals.
- It activates your subconscious mind to create solutions for getting the goals you want. You will start waking up in the morning with new ideas. You will find yourself having ideas in the shower, while you are taking long walks, and while you are driving to work.
- It creates new levels of motivation. You will start to notice you are unexpectedly doing things that take you to your goal. All of a sudden, you are raising your hand in class, volunteering to take on new assignments at work, spending out at staff meetings, asking more directly for what you want, saving money for the things that you want, paying down a credit card debt, or taking

more risks in your personal life.

Let's take a closer look at how the RAS works. At any one time, there are about 8 million bits of information streaming into your brain – most of which you cannot attend to, nor do you need to. So your brain's RAS filters most of them out, letting into your awareness only those signals that can help you survive and achieve your most important goals.

So how does your RAS know what to let in and what to filter out? It lets in anything that will help you achieve the goals you have set and constantly visualize and affirm. It also lets in anything that matches your beliefs and images about yourself, others, and the world.

The RAS is a powerful tool, but it can only look for ways to achieve the exact picture you give it. Your creative subconscious mind doesn't think in words – it can only think in pictures. So how does this help your effort to become successful and achieve the life of your dreams?

The process of visualizing for success is really quite simple. All you have to do is close your eyes and see your goals as already complete.

Add sounds and feelings to the pictures.

Fuel your images with emotion.

Start now!

Some psychologists claim that one hour of visualization is worth 7 hours of physical effort. That's a tall claim, but it makes an important point – visualization in one of the strongest tools in your success toolbox. Make sure you see it.

You don't need to visualize your future achievements for a whole hour. Just 10 to 15 minutes is plenty.

As I conceptualized my venture, I always visualized myself as respected entrepreneur who changed the way car service is perceived in the city. I visualized myself as a well know person in the city, having a reputation of honesty and integrity in my business. In the last 9 years that my venture is running I achieved exactly that what I had been visualizing. Though I acknowledge that is just the beginning and there are greater heights to achieve.

Through my life story, my failed business experiences, and all knowledge and skills that I acquired through the University of Life, I now formally coach startups, entrepreneurs and individuals. Now I conduct seminars, coach people on life transformation and business growth with different programs that I have personally developed and curated.

The people whom I coached have experienced massive transformation in their lives and businesses by taking actions on the things learnt. People who were depressed and even attempted suicides are now leading happy lives which were possible through my transformation programs.

I visualize myself with the following things:

- Driving my dream car
- Owning my dream farm house
- Being A Game Changer in the Car Service Industry
- Delivering my TED talk in India and abroad
- A successful author
- A successful life coach
- A successful business coach

ACT AS IF

Believe and act as if it were impossible to fail.

To fly as fast as thought, to be anywhere there is, you must first begin by knowing that you have already arrived.

Be, do, and have everything you want... starting now...

You can begin right now to act as if you have already achieved any goal you desire, and that outer experience of acting as if will create the inner experience – the millionaire mindset, as it were that will take you to the actual manifestation of that experience.

Remember the proper order of things is to start now and be who you want to be then do the actions that go along with being that person and soon you will find that you easily have everything you want in life – health, wealth and fulfilling relationship.

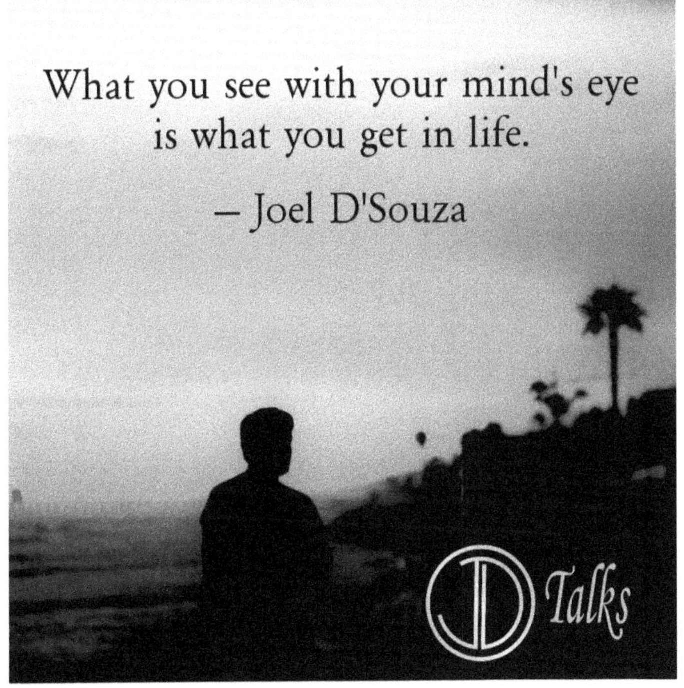

CHAPTER FIFTEEN

COMMIT TO CONSTANT LEARNING & IMPROVEMENT

We have an innate desire to endlessly learn, grow, and develop. We want to become more than what we already are. Once we yield to this inclination for continuous and never ending improvement, we lead a life of endless accomplishments and satisfaction.

He who stops being better, stops being good.

One of life's realities is that major improvements take time, they don't happen overnight.

KEEP YOUR EYES ON THE PRIZE

It's easy to be negative and unmotivated, but it takes some work to be positive and motivated. While there's no off button for those relentless "tapes" there are things that you can do to turn down the volume and shift your focus from the negative to the positive.

Successful people maintain a positive focus in life no matter what is going on around them. They stay focused on their past successes rather than their past failures, and on the next action steps they need to take to get them closer to the fulfillment of their goals rather than all the other distractions that life presents to them. They are constantly proactive in the pursuits of their chosen objectives.

An important part of any focusing regimen is to set aside time at the end of the day - just before going to sleep - to acknowledge your successes, review your goals, focus on your successful future, and make specific plans for what you want to accomplish the next day.

Why do I suggest the end of the day? Because whatever you read, see, listen to, talk about, and experience during the last 45 minutes of the day has a huge influence on your sleep and your next day. During the night your unconscious mind replays and processes this late night input up to six times more often than anything else you experienced during the day.

ARE YOU INTERESTED OR ARE YOU COMMITTED? MAKE A COMMITMENT CONTRACT

A commitment contract is a written agreement that makes it mandatory for you to perform the said actions in order to achieve the desired result.

There are three factors to be considered when you make a commitment contract. -

1. The first one is to define a goal, a target or a set of desired result. This has to be very clear, specific and unambiguously phrased.
2. The second one is to put something at stake that matters greatly to you. This could be something quantifiable or

measurable, whose loss you will deeply regret. Or, it could be something emotional and intangible like love, respect or friendship.

3. The third factor is to appoint a mentor who will review your performance and hold you responsible for your actions. You will give this person an actual piece of paper with the clauses of the 'commitment contract' specifying what you have committed yourself to achieving and what you are liable to lose if you fail to achieve it.

You realize and understand what you are doing here, don't you? When we make a commitment in our mind, we don't really articulate what we are committing to do or express how serious or important it is. When you make a commitment on paper, define what you are going to achieve and put something of value at stake, you are demonstrating your intention of sticking to your commitment.

Well, commitments are made on the basis of trust, and we assume that eventually, your conscience will get the better of you if you don't confess to an act of omission.

SUCCESS STARTS NOW. START NOW... JUST DO IT

No amount of reading or memorizing will make you successful in life. It is the understanding and application of wise thought which counts.

Many people die with their music still in them. Why is this so? Too often it is because they are always getting ready to live. Before they know it, time runs out.

First you jump off the cliff and you build wings on the way down.

A journey of 1,000 kilometers must begin with one step.

The key to success is to take what you have learned and put it into action.

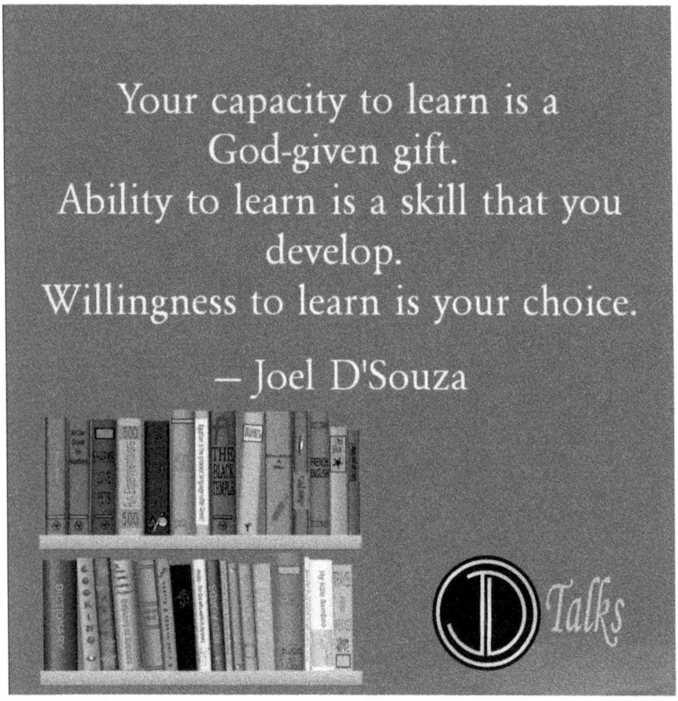

EXPRESS AUTOCARE – my childhood dream venture, a disruptive game changer in the car service industry has given me recognition that perhaps no other thing could give.

Looking back, I can honestly say that I wouldn't change a thing in my life. There have been highs and there have been terrible lows. But what mattered is the resilience I built in the face of crisis. All my experiences made me what I am today, getting stronger by the day. I live on to take life's challenges head on ...

I am thankful to each and every one in my life for what they have done for me – both good and bad.

EMPOWER YOURSELF BY EMPOWERING OTHERS

If your actions create a legacy that inspires others to dream more, learn more, do more and become more, then you are an excellent leader.

If you thoroughly know anything, teach it to others.

One of the most powerful ways to learn anything is to teach it to others. It forces you to clarify your ideas, confront inconsistencies in your own thinking, and more closely walk your talk. But most importantly, it requires you to read, study and speak the information over and over again. The resulting repetition reinforces your own learning.

TEACH THESE PRINCIPLES TO OTHERS. WHEN YOU LIFT UP OTHERS, THEY WILL LIFT YOU UP.

In conclusion of my story, I would like to say a few power phrases that keep me pushing:

- Everything you want is on the other side of fear.
- Some of the finest things in life are hidden behind our conditioned mind.
- Life is inherently risky. There is only one big risk that you should avoid at all costs – the risk of not doing things because it is risky.
- Rock bottoms in life will teach you things mountain tops cannot.
- You cannot change the people around you, but you can change the people you choose to be around.
- Pain is temporary, quitting lasts forever...

Be thankful for your struggles and pains because without it you wouldn't have known your strengths. Count your current blessings and change your perspective and you will know how beautiful life is.

– Joel D'Souza

Acknowlegdments

I have made every effort to include my dearest family and friends in my expressions of gratitude throughout my life's journey. I am deeply thankful to them.

I am grateful foremost to the Divine Creator Jehovah God for helping me and holding my hand throughout my life.

I am grateful to many people in my life the most being my wife Lydia, my father Late Daniel & my mother Leena, my siblings Allen & Benita, my in-laws Timothy & Felcy, my great friends and some who inspired me all my life through.

My uncles - Boniface & Denis and aunts - Julie & Gloria

My friends - Aju Oommen, Lionel O'Hara, Late Gills Baretto, Janet Baretto, Adrian Connor, Peter Thombre, Samson Reddimalla, Merita Reddimalla, Datta Thorat, Dr. Ashissh Jain, Venus Joy, Tushar Jain, Gopal Hegde, Dhiraj Hegde, Aparna Garge & Anant Singh.

My inspiration & mentors - My Late Father Daniel D'Souza, my ex-boss Tushar Mehta, Dr. Abhay Upasani, Cricketers Sachin Tendulkar and Rahul Dravid.

My support system - My Family, My Team at Express Autocare & My Business Associates.

This book contains extracts from the following authors & their books which inspired me and helped me transform my life – Santosh Nair (Eleven Commandments of Life Maximization), Jack Canfield (Success Principles)

www.ingramcontent.com/pod-product-compliance
Lightning Source LLC
LaVergne TN
LVHW021142160826
845679LV00023B/2011